Saint Mary's University

An Anniversary Portrait

Anne West

Saint Mary's University
A CELEBRATION 1802·2002

Saint Mary's University
Halifax, Nova Scotia, Canada

Community Books
Lockeport, Nova Scotia

Design: Brenda Conroy
Front cover photograph: Don Robinson
Back cover photographs: Paul Fitzgerald, Sandor Fizli and Lisa Legatto
Author photograph, inside back cover: Photo 67
Printed and bound in Canada by Hignell Printing

Copies of this book may be obtained from:
University Bookstore
Saint Mary's University, Halifax, NS, B3H 3C3
Tel: (902) 496-8765, e-mail: bookstore@stmarys.ca

Published by Saint Mary's University, Halifax, Nova Scotia
and
Community Books
RR #1 Lockeport Nova Scotia B0T 1L0
Ph/fax (902) 656-2223
kathleen.tudor@ns.sympatico.ca
www.selfpublishingspecialists.com

National Library of Canada Cataloguing in Publication

West, Anne

Saint Mary's University : an anniversary portrait / Anne West.

ISBN 1-896496-34-2

1. Saint Mary's University (Halifax, N.S.)—History. 2. Saint Mary's University (Halifax, N.S.) —Pictorial works. I. Title.

LE3.S59W48 2002 378.716'225 C2002-902639-3

Contents

Letter from the President 5
Acknowledgements 6

Part One: Evolution
Bishop Burke's Vision, 1802–1913 7
The Irish Christian Brothers, 1913–1940 15
The Jesuit Years, 1940–1970 31
Athletics: The Jesuit Years 55
Saint Mary's High School 63
A Public University 69
Athletics: The Public University 95

Part Two: Snapshots of Saint Mary's
The Academic Year Unfolds 113
Teaching and Learning 125
Campus Life 133
A Family Affair 149

This Anniversary Portrait *is dedicated to those who in the past held true, to those who hold true today and to those who in the future will hold true to Saint Mary's commitment to excellence in teaching and research, accessibility, outreach to all communities and fiscal responsibility.*

The 200th Anniversary Committee

Charles (Chuck) Bridges, Chair

Hon. Helen Gillis, Vice-Chair

Dr. Elizabeth A. Chard, Vice-Chair

Heather M. Fitzpatrick

Keith Hotchkiss

Joanne Byrne

Wendy Brookhouse

Barry Gallant

Heather Harris

Rob Finn

Paul Deveau

Dr. Terry Murphy

Carol Dodds

Samantha Anderson

Peter Halpin

Stephanie Babcock

Dr. Cyril Byrne

Dana Clements

Gordon Laurin

Dr. David Richardson

Kathy Mullane

Dr. Colin Dodds

Denis Leclaire

Alison Whiteman

Robert Belliveau, QC, Chair, Board of Governors (retiring July 2002)

Paul Dyer, Chair, Board of Governors

With special thanks to Dr. Terence R.B. Donahoe, QC, and the Hon. Alan R. Abraham, CM.

Letter from the President

Dear Santamarians and Friends of Saint Mary's University,

Saint Mary's University is a product of its rich history—a history driven by its people. This book, *An Anniversary Portrait,* brings to life the people who have been part of that history in many different capacities. It is a poignant reflection of Saint Mary's past as the University celebrates its 200th anniversary, and also a guide to welcome our future.

Saint Mary's earliest beginnings can be traced to Reverend Edmund Burke, Vicar General of Nova Scotia under the Roman Catholic Diocese of Quebec. In 1802, Edmund Burke initiated instruction for young men at the Glebe House on the corner of Spring Garden Road and Barrington Street. He displayed vision and persistence in the face of strenuous opposition from the establishment of the day. Without him, these students would have been denied access to higher education. Those that followed have maintained that vision and commitment and built on the foundations he laid.

From the outset, Saint Mary's served as a community resource, and in 1841, the Nova Scotia House of Assembly gave formal recognition of its academic role with degree-granting status. Although Saint Mary's has moved its physical location over the years, it has never wavered in its commitment to meeting community needs and maintaining its tradition of excellence in teaching and scholarship. Today, Saint Mary's is a dynamic, urban, interfaith university. It has a globally recognized reputation for accessibility, innovative teaching and research; and its outreach is local, regional and international.

President Dr. Colin Dodds in the classroom in the 1980s

An Anniversary Portrait uses photographs to capture 200 years at Saint Mary's. Research for a full-length history of the institution is now being undertaken and will be another lasting result of this celebration.

I hope that this book will bring back happy memories for the alumni(ae), students, faculty, staff and friends who make up the Saint Mary's family. As the University embarks on its third century, lest we forget, it provides a lasting record of everyone's place in the evolution of our beloved Saint Mary's.

Sincerely

Colin Dodds, President

Acknowledgements

So many people helped me give birth to this book. It would not have been possible without the advice and support of Dr. John Reid, who helped me struggle through the difficult days and also prevented me from making any serious historical howlers. Dr. Cyril Byrne shared with me his inexhaustible fund of knowledge about the Irish connection and University Archivist Anne MacLean and her student staff helped me with unfailing patience, kindness and efficiency. I'm also grateful to Karen White, archivist of the Archdiocese of Halifax, Garry Shutlak of Nova Scotia Archives and Record Management, David Flemming who gave invaluable help with the High School section and Brother J.B. D'Arcy of the Christian Brothers of Ireland in St. John's, Newfoundland. Other Santamarians whose help was invaluable include Dr. Kenneth Ozmon, Dr. Elizabeth A. Chard, Kevin Cleary, Don Keleher and Edmund Boyd (whose roots are Santamarian). I'm grateful to Chuck Bridges for giving me the chance to try and to the staff of the Public Affairs Department for so much help. When it came to athletics, I would have been dead in the water without Bob Hayes who did everything he could to help and told me great stories in the process, Doug Wright, who gave me access to Saint Mary's Sports Hall of Fame photograhs, Terry O'Neil who provided advice and photographs from the Halifax Herald and Al Hollingsworth who actually wrote the sports sections. I am also grateful to Chris Murphy for the use of his notes for a history of the institution, to Darrell Freeman for the design concept, to designer Brenda Conroy for turning a pile of photographs into an exciting story and to Joan Dawson, whose meticulous proofreading and grammatical expertise kept it literate. Finally, to my husband Chris for living through yet another huge project; this time one which put the dining table out of use for nine months.

Photographs

Many of the photographs used in the book do not have the names of the photographers on them. However, I know that the work of the following is included and thank them: Don Robinson, Photo 67, Wambolt-Waterfield, Clark Photographic, Peter Parsons, Elizabeth Stevens, Dr. Keith Vaughan, Lisa Legatto, Paul Fitzgerald, Herald Photo, Gauvin & Gentzell and many unknown photographers. Thanks also to the Archdiocese of Halifax for permission to use photographs from its archives, to the family of Bob Chambers for allowing us to use the cartoon on page 70, to Marilyn Gurney of Maritime Command Museum for permission to use the 1917 photograph on page 19, to Nova Scotia Archives and Record Management for permission to reproduce the Notman photograph on page 11, the 1917 Explosion photo on page 19 and the section of Hopkins's *Atlas of Halifax* on page 11, to Margaret Enright for permission to use the photograph of her father Lance Corporal Donaghue on page 18, to the family of J. Wallace Foley for use of photographs on pages 42 and 46, and to the Museum of Industry in Stellarton, N.S., for permission to photograph the computer on page 33.

Anne West

The author, former Assistant Director of Public Affairs Anne West, with Prime Minister Kim Campbell at Saint Mary's in 1993

Saint Mary's University Archives

Saint Mary's now has an archives department and is working hard to build up its collection of historic documents, photographs and artifacts. If you can correct any of the facts in this book or have any material that would be of interest to the University, please send it to University Archives, Saint Mary's University, Halifax, Nova Scotia, B3H 3C3, or contact the archivist at (902) 420-5508 or archives@stmarys.ca.

Part One
Evolution

Bishop Burke's Vision 1802–1913

In 1801, Reverend Edmund Burke arrived in Halifax as vicar general of Nova Scotia. He had been sent to Nova Scotia, which was part of the huge Roman Catholic diocese of Québec, by the Bishop of Québec. In Halifax he found a 52-year-old British colony with a large Irish population worshipping in a small wooden church on Spring Garden Road, close to Barrington Street. It had been built in 1784 and was dedicated to Saint Peter.

Burke also found a congregation which had no schools where its children could be taught in the Roman Catholic faith. The Church of England was the established church in Nova Scotia, and in 1766 legislation

Reverend Edmund Burke, the first bishop of Nova Scotia

had been passed forbidding Catholics to set up schools. This was repealed in 1786, but the political climate of the city was not favourable to the development of the aspirations of the Roman Catholic population.

Father Burke moved fast. Early in 1802, he petitioned the House of Assembly to incorporate an act giving permission to open a school for Catholic boys. Opposition stalled the request, but Burke went ahead, raised funds from the Charitable Irish Society and other sources, and built a school on the corner of Spring Garden Road and Barrington Street. Anti-Catholic elements worked against Burke. He was not granted a licence for his school, so the building was used as the Glebe House of the parish and Burke rented out the lower part of it to Lawrence Doyle, a Halifax merchant. Undeterred, Burke began to provide an informal Catholic education for a few young men in his house, and 1802 is recognized as the founding date of Saint Mary's University.

During this period, Halifax was enlivened by a war of words between Burke and his

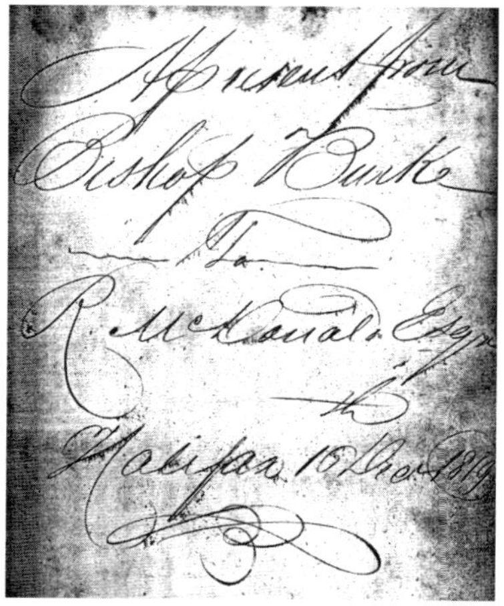

Above: "A present from Bishop Burke to R. McDonald Esq., Halifax, 16 Dec., 1819." This dedication in Bishop Burke's handwriting appears in a copy of his book *First Principles of Christianity*, printed in Halifax by John Howe and Son in 1810.

Below: Etching of Saint Peter's and Glebe House (No drawing exists of the first chapel; this is the 1820 stone church.)

Lithograph of Colonel John Burke

chief adversary, Irish-born Bishop Charles Inglis, first Anglican bishop of Nova Scotia, who was strongly anti-Catholic.

In 1806, a licence for a school was finally granted, thanks to the intervention of 23-year-old Colonel John Burke, who had arrived in the colony in command of the 98th Regiment. This well-connected Roman Catholic Irishman exercised his considerable charm and political influence on Governor Sir John Wentworth and, in Father Burke's words, "...the business was done in an instant." But Burke's troubles were not over and he was unable to obtain priests to help him in this work, despite searches in the United States and Europe. He determined that a home-grown clergy was the only hope.

In 1817, Nova Scotia was separated from the diocese of Québec, and in the following year Burke was consecrated bishop.

In 1818, Bishop Burke took four young men into his home in the college building on Spring Garden and Barrington to train for holy orders. In the same year two of these seminarians oversaw a boys' school in the same building and he also started a girls' school. His first two "graduates" were ordained in June 1819. By September 1820, there were 193 girls and about 100 boys attending Burke's schools.

In 1820, construction began on a fine stone cathedral for the new diocese to replace the small wooden church. It came into use in 1829 and was again dedicated to Saint Peter. In 1833 it was rededicated to Saint Mary at the request of Bishop William Fraser.

Bishop Burke died in 1820 and a successor was not consecrated until 1827. During the *interregnum*, Burke's nephew John Carroll, an 1820 graduate of the college, acted as administrator for the diocese. The new bishop, Reverend William Fraser, a Scot who elected to run the diocese from Antigonish, did not support the idea of a college in Halifax; it closed and candidates for holy orders and would-be members of the lay professions were educated in Québec or abroad.

During the late 1830s, great activity took place in the field of higher education. Dalhousie, stillborn in 1818, reopened in 1838. Queen's (Acadia) was founded by the Baptists in 1838. The Irish Catholics of Halifax were still anxious to provide a suitable education for their sons and, also in 1838, a group from Saint Mary's Cathedral petitioned Bishop Fraser to obtain priests to re-establish Bishop Burke's college. This group included Warden Lawrence O'Connor Doyle, who was born in Bishop Burke's house in 1804, when his parents were renting part of it. He had been sent to England to be educated two years before Burke admitted the first students to his college, and became the first Catholic to practise law in British North America.

In 1839, the newly-ordained priest Father Richard Baptist O'Brien arrived in Halifax from Ireland to run the college. In 1840, Saint Mary's College opened in a new building on Grafton Street with an enrolment of 70 to 80 pupils. In 1841, it was incorporated and given degree-granting powers for 11 years. With this charter came funding from the province—a grant of $1,622 per annum for the next four years.

The College was widely advertised in places which had large Irish-Catholic populations. A prospectus published in the *Boston Pilot* of February 1, 1840, states that "No pains shall be spared in the effort to bestow upon the pupil, the profession, learned or commercial, for which he may be intended and the GREAT END to which all human improvement should be directed." The curriculum included English, Spanish, French, Latin, Greek and Hebrew. A course of natural philosophy included algebra, geometry, trigonometry, mechanics, astronomy, hydrostatics, pneumatics, electricity and galvanism; arithmetic, book-keeping, geography, history, etc. A class of moral philosophy was to follow shortly for aspirants to holy orders. No requirement was ever made for a declaration of faith.

In 1844, the diocese was divided into two sections. Bishop Fraser remained in Antigonish as Bishop of Arichat and an apostolic administrator was appointed for Halifax.

In 1845, Father O'Brien returned to Ireland. With his departure the Vicar General of the diocese, Thomas Connolly, became president. His college had 80 students in 1851 and he boasted to Joseph Howe that Nova Scotia had 20 to 30 professional men who owed

Left: Lawrence O'Connor Doyle

Above: Father Patrick Power

Below: Father Richard Baptist O'Brien, a miniature by William Valentine

their higher studies to the College. In 1852, the College was given permanent degree-granting powers. But funding remained a problem and a succession of diocesan priests struggled to maintain the institution. Between 1852 and 1868, Saint Mary's had six chief administrators, but managed to keep going.

In 1852, in response to worsening relations between the Irish Catholics of Halifax and the Scottish Catholics of eastern Nova Scotia, Halifax was made an archdiocese, creating an ecclesiastical province with four dioceses, Halifax, Arichat, Saint John and Charlottetown.

Hopkins' *Atlas of Halifax* (1878) showing the Bel-Air estate just east of Gottingen Street. It originally extended as far as Agricola Street.

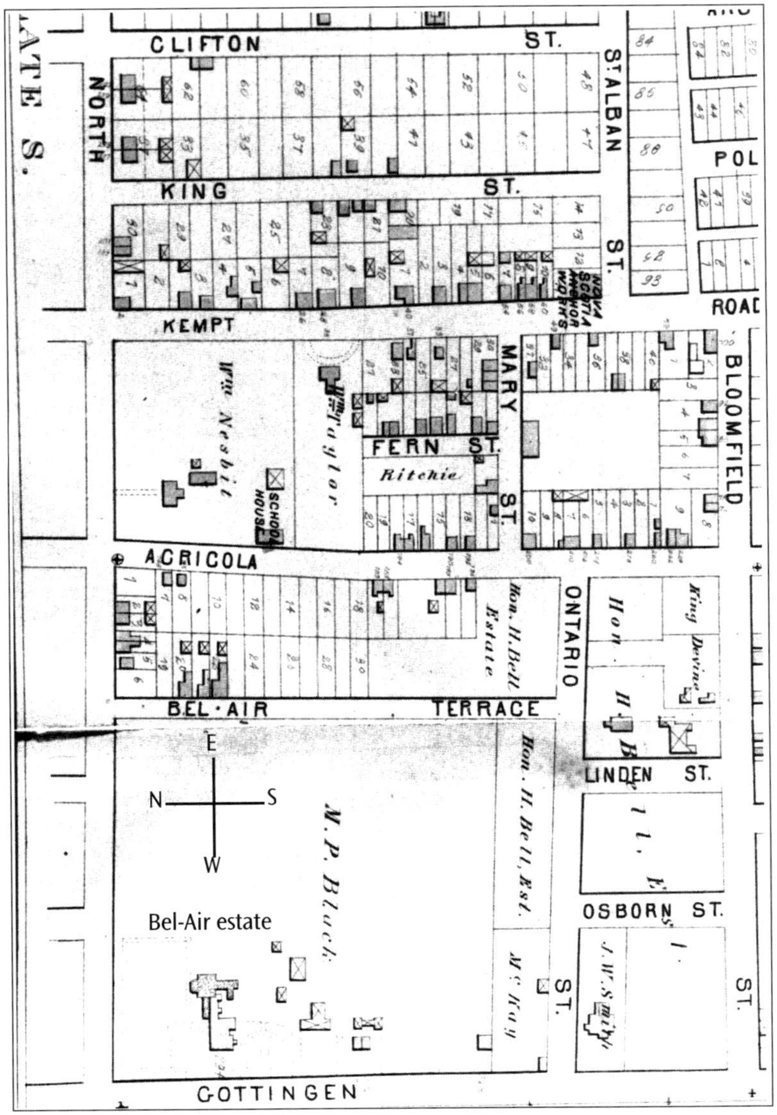

Father Patrick Power became the first Nova Scotia-born head of the College in 1853. Born in 1828, he was one of the first students enrolled at Saint Mary's under Father O'Brien. He was ordained in July 1851 and spent his entire ministry in connection with Saint Mary's parish or College. Father Power was director of the College from 1853 to 1855 and its president from 1859 to 1862.

In 1868, teaching duties at Saint Mary's were taken over by the Christian Brothers of Saint John the Baptist de la Salle, who moved the College to the Bel-Air estate off Agricola Street. Their tenure was short, but the fine pupils they trained included William McCarthy, future archbishop of Halifax, Peter O'Hearn, long-time principal of Saint Patrick's Boys' School and Martin Griffin, editor of the *Halifax Herald* and *Toronto Mail* and ultimately Canadian Parliamentary Librarian. The brothers recognized the importance of trade to the area and introduced a commercial course.

Rev. Edward Francis Murphy 1876–1877

In 1876, as the result of a dispute between the archdiocese and the order, the Christian Brothers left Halifax without notice. The College was taken over by the archdiocese. Reverend Edward Francis Murphy served as president until the following year, and it was moved to a location on Barrington Street, near Tobin Street. Enrolment at this time

Reverend Richard Kearns

was between 30 and 50.

In 1876, the *University Act* was passed, creating one University of Halifax with the colleges of Acadia, Dalhousie, King's, Mount Allison, St. Francis Xavier and Saint Mary's. In 1878 and 1879, degrees were conferred in the name of the University of Halifax. In 1881, the University of Halifax ceased to exist, government grants to the colleges were stopped and Saint Mary's College closed due to lack of funds and teachers. Reverend Richard Kearns, an Irishman who first came to Nova Scotia in 1865, became president of Saint Mary's in September 1877 and presided over this difficult period of its history "with great credit to himself and to those under his instruction."

Also in 1881, wealthy Halifax merchant Patrick Power died, leaving a sizeable bequest for a boys' college. However, his will stipulated that to be eligible for the bequest, the college must be run by the Jesuits. No order of Jesuits was willing to come to Halifax, nor were the Benedictines, so the bequest could not be used. In the late 1880s, Archbishop Cornelius O'Brien again approached the Jesuits and the Benedictines, together with the Christian Brothers, but all declined, so the funds of the Patrick Power Estate remained out of reach until 1913.

Since his arrival in the city as Archbishop of Halifax in 1882, Reverend Dr. Cornelius O'Brien had seen the reopening of Saint Mary's as key to maintaining the growing social status of Catholics. Between 1888 and 1898, an American branch of the La Salle Christian Brothers ran the La Salle Academy on South and then Barrington streets. They did not grant degrees under Saint Mary's charter and so are only indirectly part of this story.

By the turn of the 20th century, 20 years had passed during which no Catholic higher education was available in Halifax for men. The reopening of Saint Mary's had become Archbishop O'Brien's obsession. He made several attempts to access the Patrick Power Estate but the executors refused to release funds for a college not run by Jesuits. Finally he sought recourse in the law and began a civil suit. He was so convinced that his claim was in accordance with Patrick Power's intentions that he went ahead with his plans. In 1902, a 15-acre campus on Windsor Street at Quinpool road was pur-

Below: Halifax merchant and benefactor Patrick Power and his wife Ellen

chased and the Eudist Fathers were approached to provide teaching services.

Many of the lay members of the diocese felt this project was doomed to failure and did not respond well to Archbishop O'Brien's appeals for funds. It was only by draining his own bank account that he was able to fulfil his dream. The cornerstone was laid on July 2, 1903, and the new "collegiate school" opened on September 21, 1903 as a pre-college institution with two classes of 24 pupil taught by two lay professors.

O'Brien had won his case against the Patrick Power Estate before two courts in Nova Scotia, but, just three months before Saint Mary's reopened, the decision was overturned by the Supreme Court of Canada. The new college stood on shifting financial sands. Archbishop O'Brien continued to devote much effort to raising funds for the boarding facility which he felt essential to its success. This time he could not afford a general contractor and so himself supervised the work of converting a private residence next to the college.

Above: The campus at Windsor Street and Quinpool Road

Right: The man who made it happen—Reverend Dr. Cornelius O'Brien

Boarders were accepted in 1905.

The archdiocese patently could not afford such an ambitious school; it operated on a shoestring and some faculty members were let go. Father McManus, who was president of the College from 1905 to 1913, had to study commerce by night at Dalhousie in order to teach it by day at Saint Mary's. Surprisingly, however, fundraising began in 1909 to add a new front section to the Windsor Street building. It was to contain classrooms, laboratories, a library and a large dormitory, but it did not happen. By 1912–13 enrolment was only 53. It seemed Saint Mary's would have to close again.

Archbishop O'Brien was succeeded by Reverend Edward McCarthy, a native Haligonian and a graduate of Saint Mary's. With his encouragement, Halifax Catholics began to take a deeper interest in the growth of the College and the local Knights of Columbus petitioned the Superior General of the Christian Brothers of Ireland for a community of brothers for Saint Mary's. After lengthy negotiations with Brother P.J. Hennessey, Assistant General of the order, a contract was signed on May 30, 1913, giving the Irish Christian Brothers management of Saint Mary's. The Knights of Columbus organized a lightning fundraising campaign, which provided $47,000 to build a new wing and renovate the College in preparation for the arrival of the Brothers.

Father Charles McManus

NEW FRONT ST. MARY'S COLLEGE

Above: Rev. Edward McCarthy (later Archbishop)

Left: 1909 drawing of proposed new wing for Windsor Street

The Irish Christian Brothers 1913–1940

The Irish Christian Brothers

In 1913, the Irish Christian Brothers became the teaching order at Saint Mary's. The executors of Patrick Power's estate finally agreed to grant the money from his bequest for the use of this new administration. Under the care of the Brothers, the High School and College grew, and new courses were added to meet the needs of a changing world.

Previous page: Brother P.J. Hennessey (Assistant General), who negotiated the coming of the order, visited Halifax in 1915. This photograph commemorates the event. L to R, Front: Br. P.J. Culhane (president 1913 to 1919 and 1922 to 1925), Br. Hennessey, Br. Charles McManus. Back: Br. W. Cornelia (president 1931 to 1937), Br. M.G. Grangel (?), Br. J.V. Birmingham.

Below: Class photograph 1915. L to R, Front: Clair Hayes, Tom Stokes; Middle: Dr. Herbert Corbett, John Moore, n/k, Brother McCarthy, Dr. Walter Keating, Mel Hawes, Tom Kerr; Back: Roy Campbell, John Martin, Gerald Flavin, Admiral Grace Crosley (?), Dr. Ed. Granville, Rev. Monsignor Leo Murphy, Eddie Donahoe, Neil Flannery.

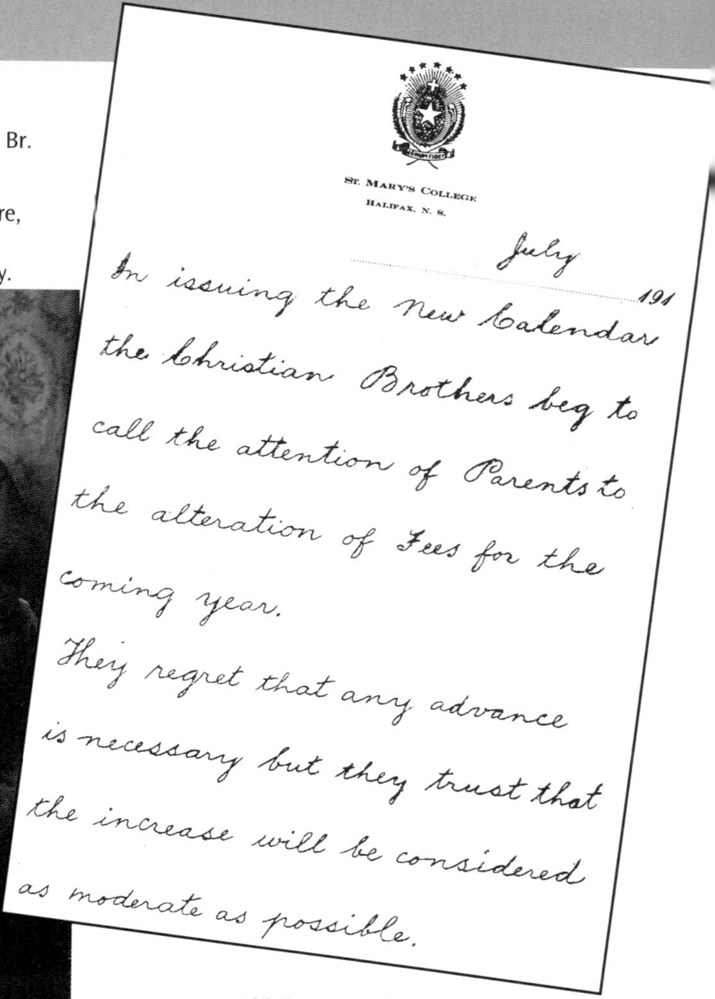

ST. MARY'S COLLEGE
HALIFAX, N. S.

July 191

In issuing the New Calendar the Christian Brothers beg to call the attention of Parents to the alteration of Fees for the coming year.

They regret that any advance is necessary but they trust that the increase will be considered as moderate as possible.

This letter was found in a 1912–13 copy of the Academic Calendar.

Degrees again

The Calendar for 1912–13 reveals that no degree courses had been offered since the reopening of the College in 1903, and that an Arts course leading to a Bachelor of Arts was beginning that year. Subjects offered at the university level were philosophy, Latin, Greek, French, English, trigonometry, geometry, calculus, algebra, chemistry, physics and religion.

Arts graduates in 1930. L to R, Front: Edward O'Connor (later Br.), Arthur Sheehan, James W. Dwyer, Walter D. O'Hearn, William R. Murphy. Centre: Br. P.J. Culhane, Br. C. Stirling (President). Back: Br. M.F. Garvey, Br. C.A. Lynam, n/k, Br. A.L. Pakenham.

Below: Fees seem modest today, especially $3 a year for the use of a typewriter.

TERMS

The school year is divided into three terms:

BOARDERS.

1st or September Term:	
From opening until Christmas Vacation	$ 60 00
2nd or January Term:	
From Christmas Vacation until Easter	60 00
3rd or April Term:	
From Easter Vacation until Closing in June	40 00
	$160 00

This sum pays for full board, tuition and washing.

Non-boarders will be charged as heretofore:

For 1st Term	$18 00
2nd "	18 00
3rd "	14 00
	$50 00

OPTIONAL FEES.

Physical Drill, 1st and 2nd term, each	$ 1 50
Physical Drill, 3rd term	1 00
Use of Typewriter, each term	1 00
Piano Lessons, with use of instrument, each term	10 00
Private rooms, per year	20 00

These fees are in all cases exacted in advance of the term. No reduction will be made for students who enter late or leave before the end of the term.

The war to end all wars, 1914–1918

Some Santamarians must have taken part in the First World War. No College journals were published during this period, so we know little about the participants. One, however, was Lance-Corporal John Cameron Donaghue, born in 1896. He received the Military Medal after the battle of Passchendaele in 1917 for holding a foxhole single-handed for 48 hours after his comrades had been killed. He lost a leg, but lived to tell the tale to his children.

Corporal John Cameron Donaghue

Explosion

Early on December 5, 1917, what was then the largest ever man-made explosion rocked Halifax when the *Imo* and the *Mont Blanc* collided in the harbour. Archbishop McCarthy offered Saint Mary's College as an emergency hospital. He advised that the "15 Christian Brothers of Ireland in residence would assist or vacate as deemed best." Quickly, 138 beds were set up and the building was used until January 15, 1918, first by a Boston medical team, then by the Rhode Island Red Cross.

Right: Archbishop Edward J. McCarthy

Below: Arthur F. Inglis, a 21-year-old engineering student in 1917, was on his way to the College when the explosion took place. Saint Mary's celebrated his 95th birthday in 1991, when he was believed to be its oldest living alumnus. L ro R: Dr. Kenneth Ozmon, President, Arthur Inglis, Robert Hessian, student.

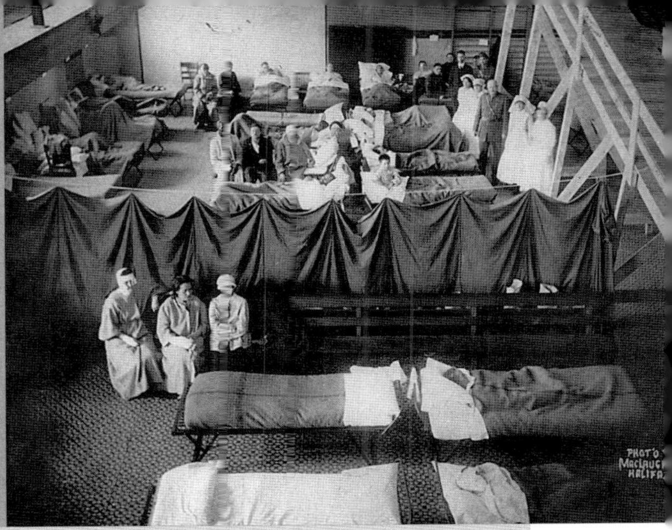

Right: The YMCA on Barrington Street was also turned into an emergency hospital.

Below: Medical personnel in front of the college

An engineering diploma

The Irish Christian Brothers worked hard to provide the type of education needed by young men at this time. They introduced commercial subjects and, in 1916, set up a three-year Engineering Diploma leading to a two-year Bachelor of Engineering course at the Nova Scotia Technical College.

Left: These Arts and Engineering students from 1919–1920 included Saint Mary's first Engineering graduates.

Below: A later Engineering class

A University of the Maritime Provinces

A 1922 report commissioned by the Carnegie Corporation of New York recommended that all the principal "institutions of higher learning" in the Maritimes should move to Halifax to form a federated "University of the Maritime Provinces." Although the Carnegie Corporation offered to underwrite the cost of removal, the only practical result was the relocation of the University of King's College from Windsor. Pope Pius XI declared in 1923 that no Catholic colleges should enter the proposed federation. The Catholic institutions withdrew and eventually the idea was abandoned.

Above left: An informal group of graduates in the spring of 1928

Above right: Snappy hats feature in this casual student group with Brother Garvey in October 1927.

Right: Class photo for 1926–27

A Roman Catholic institution

The Irish Christian Brothers ran a truly religious institution, as is clear from the pages of *The Collegian*. A number of their students discovered a vocation and went on to join the priesthood.

The College was the venue for the 3rd Annual Catholic Students' Crusade, AD 1927.

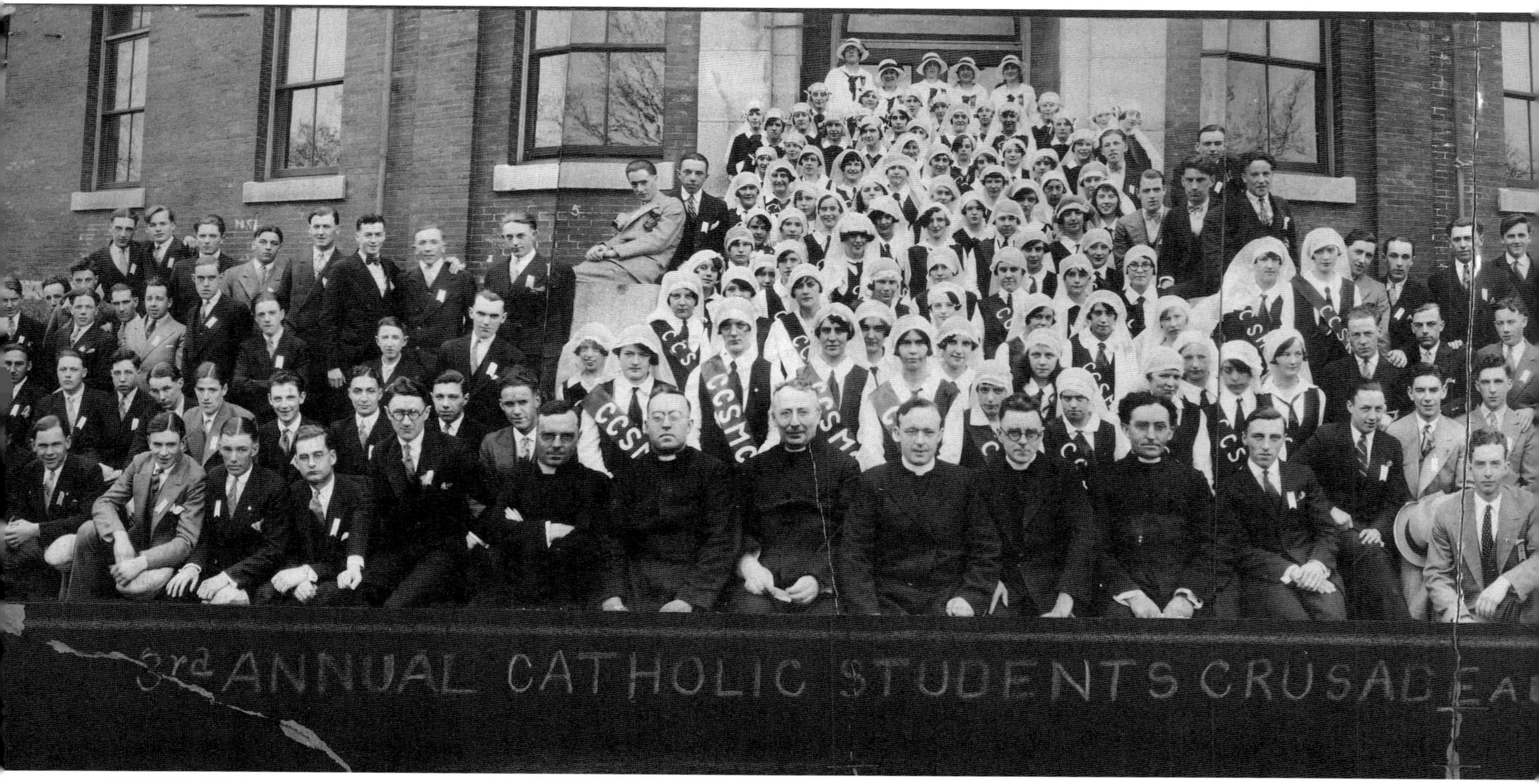

"AGE QUOD AGIS"

To live as nobly as I can;
To be, no matter where, a man;
To take what comes of good or ill;
To cling to Faith and Honour still;
To do my best, and let that stand
The record of my brain and hand.

The Collegian was revived in 1924. As well as this poem about the College motto, *Age Quod Agis*, the February 1925 issue included articles about the Holy Name Society and the Martyr Priests of Canada.

This early 1920s class photo includes two Santamarians who went into the church, Monsignor William Burns (fourth from left, back) and Rev. H. Durney (sixth from left, back). It also includes Gerald Hayes (fourth from left front) "revered teacher at St. Patrick's Boys High" and William Finn (fifth from left, back).

The Patrick Power connection

Mrs. Eileen Donahoe is the great granddaughter of benefactor Patrick Power. Her husband, Senator Richard Donahoe, who was a trustee of the Patrick Power estate, attended Saint Mary's High School and College in the 1930s and, in the late 1930s, was the first person to teach political science there.

All the world's a stage

Life had its lighter side. Music, drama and debating were among the extra-curricular activities promoted by the Irish Christian Brothers at both the college and high school level.

This 1916–1917 play seems to focus on a wartime theme. A nurse stands on the right and could the young man be a deserter?

Above left: Napoleon perhaps?

Above right: A 1922–23 production

Right: The stars of Hamlet in 1920 included (L to R) W.J. Burns, William Finn, n/k, and Gerald Godsoe. William Finn and W.J. Burns also appear in the class photo on page 23.

Mens sana in corpore sano *(A healthy mind in a healthy body)*

Edwardian educators believed strongly that a healthy body would result in a healthy mind, and this philosophy was enshrined in the program of Saint Mary's High School and College. In 1908, when the first edition of *The Collegian* appeared, sport was already a well established and important part of the curriculum.

Top: The 1921 Field Day included a five-mile road race.

Above: Exercise with Indian clubs

Left: This fine set piece was part of a 1920s gymnastics display.

Winning Santamarians

By the early 1920s, the pages of *The Santamarian* were peppered with team photographs of city and provincial champions in hockey, track, football (soccer) and basketball. Lacrosse, road racing (bicycles) and gymnastics were also encouraged by the Irish Christian Brothers.

Saint Mary's basketball team, 1926–1927

The 1930s

In 1934, a Commerce Department was established, offering degree and non-degree programs. In 1936 the student newspaper, *St. Mary's Journal,* was published for the first time.

It was the era of swing music and the Big Band, and the 1937 "orchestra," complete with bow ties and violins, also includes trumpet, trombone, traps and drums.

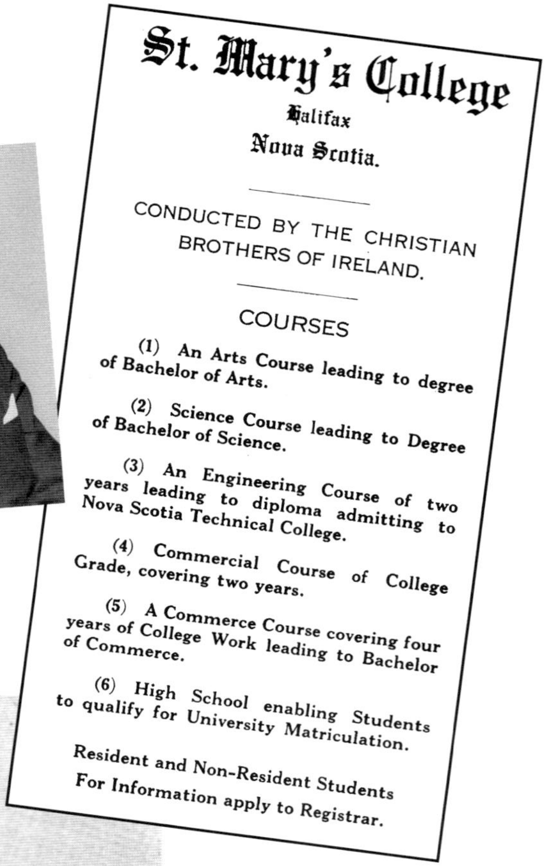

St. Mary's College
Halifax
Nova Scotia.

CONDUCTED BY THE CHRISTIAN BROTHERS OF IRELAND.

COURSES

(1) An Arts Course leading to degree of Bachelor of Arts.

(2) Science Course leading to Degree of Bachelor of Science.

(3) An Engineering Course of two years leading to diploma admitting to Nova Scotia Technical College.

(4) Commercial Course of College Grade, covering two years.

(5) A Commerce Course covering four years of College Work leading to Bachelor of Commerce.

(6) High School enabling Students to qualify for University Matriculation.

Resident and Non-Resident Students
For Information apply to Registrar.

Above left: Harold "Babe" Beazley was Saint Mary's first Commerce graduate and its first Dean of Commerce. He also coached hockey.

Above right: This prospectus from the 1935 *Collegian* includes the newly established two-year non-credit Commercial Course and the four-year Bachelor of Commerce degree. The High School is still closely woven into the fabric of the College.

Left: The "re-organized and augmented" Orchestra of Saint Mary's College, which played at the Annual Student Variety Show at the Playhouse in March 1937.

He shoots, he scores!

Left: The "Brylcreem Boys" of the 1939 hockey team

Below: The 1934–1935 hockey team won the City Intercollegiate Hockey Championship.

Football arrives

In 1933, 1,200 fans watched Halifax's first game of American Football at the Windsor Street campus of Saint Mary's. Hastily prepared by Brother O'Donnell, the determined Santamarians faced a team of American students from Dalhousie, but were beaten 13–0. Enthusiasm ran high and commentators noted that the game "might just catch on."

The shadow of war – again

In December 1934, a political essay in *The Collegian* described growing tension in Europe and predicted another world conflict. In 1937, *The Collegian* optimistically wished the newly crowned George VI "an enduring peace throughout the realm." By 1939, Saint Mary's Canadian Officers' Training Corps claimed to be nearing its goal of becoming the "most efficient unit of its kind in this Military District."

In 1939, the Technical College and Saint Mary's companies of the Canadian Officers' Training Corps posed together at Camp Petawawa, Ontario. This camp was the culminating event of a busy year of training for the 85 cadets, who also gave "an excellent display of ceremonial drill" at the annual inspection in the Armouries.

The Jesuit Years 1940–1970

Father Michael W. Burke-Gaffney, SJ, a notable scientist and astronomer, was one of the first group of Jesuits to come to Saint Mary's in 1940. He served as Dean of Engineering, Dean of Science and Professor of Astronomy, and introduced the Astronomy program in 1957. He was in demand to lecture on the Russian spacecraft *Sputnik* when it went into orbit in 1957. Saint Mary's observatory is named for him.

The Jesuit Fathers

For 30 years, priests of the Upper Canada College of the Society of Jesus ruled College and (until its 1963 demise) High School with intellectual rigour, kindness and justice. They raised academic standards and reached forward to meet the needs of a changing world. Legend has it that they ploughed their salaries back into the institution to help with running expenses.

In the 1970s, the student centre was named for two dedicated Jesuit teachers. L to R: Alumni Director Kevin Cleary, Father J.J. Hennessey, SJ, Student Services Director Bob Hayes and Father Michael J. O'Donnell, SJ.

Below: Rev. Michael W. Burke-Gaffney Observatory, opened 197

Above: Father William Stewart, SJ, taught philosophy, but played many other roles.

Right: Father Patrick G. Malone, President 1956–1959

Above right: Father Henry Labelle, SJ, the last of seven Jesuit presidents of Saint Mary's (1967–1970)

Father William Lonc, SJ, taught physics and astronomy from 1964 until retirement in 1995. He divided his time between his office in the bowels of McNally and the roof of the building, which bristles with his notable radio astronomy devices.

Larger photo: In 1994, Father Lonc hooked up a radio antenna to catch the sound of comet fragments colliding with Jupiter.

Computer on campus

In 1959, the Jesuits brought to Saint Mary's the Royal McBee LGP-30, the first electronic digital computer in the region. It was used for educational purposes, was available to local industries and can now be seen in the Museum of Industry, Stellarton, N.S.

Below: The computer

Bottom: Father John Power, SJ, (centre back) introduced High School students to the principles of computing by using the computer to play blackjack!

World War II

The *Collegian* is filled with brave young faces in uniform and notes of the decorations they received. In 1943, it records 95 alumni serving in the Air Force, 76 in the navy and 188 in the army, a total of 359. The army contingent included six reardons.

In 1939, after his freshman year at Saint Mary's, Hal Lawrence joined the Royal Canadian Navy. In August 1942, serving on the Corvette *Oakville,* he boarded and captured the crew of U-94, which sank. He received the DSC from King George VI for his part in this event. This official painting, which appeared in the 1943 *Collegian,* restores the shorts which he lost while getting aboard! Lawrence wrote about his wartime experiences in *A Bloody War.*

Santamarians served in the army, the navy and the airforce.

The home front

At home, the Canadian Officers' Training Corps had the largest enrolment in its history and the Big Band craze continued, with a 21-piece band sporting the SMC crest on their distinctly military style shirts...not a violin in sight!

Above: This is believed to be the 1941 celebration of 100 years since incorporation, although the plaque on stage looks like an honour roll.

Left: 1943, the Big Band era at Saint Mary's

Archbishop John McNally

The Jesuits were running the College, but the Archdiocese still owned it, and Archbishop McNally was in charge. John McNally was born in Ireland in 1870. He became Archbishop of Halifax in 1937, dismissed the Irish Christian Brothers and brought the Jesuits to Saint Mary's. He found the Windsor Street campus in poor shape and decided to move the College to new premises. When first proposed, the project was referred to as the Archbishop's White Elephant—nobody believed so large a building would ever be fully occupied!

Right: Archbishop McNally as Bishop of Calgary between 1913 and 1924. When fundraising for Saint Mary's became a burden to the faithful, he responded to criticism by saying that as its shepherd, he surely had a right to fleece the flock.

Right: John McNally, centre, as a young man. He died in 1952.

Opposite page: 1944 Faculty Tea hosted by the Ladies' Auxiliary. Standing L to R: Mayor J.E. Lloyd, Premier A.S. MacMillan, Very Reverend F.C. Smith, SJ (President), Mrs. J.E. Lloyd, Mrs. J.W. Dwyer, Lt. Gov. H.E. Kendall, Mrs. H.E. Kendall, His Grace Archbishop McNally, Mrs. A.S. MacMillan. Mrs. R. Bell and Mrs. H.H. Millar poured.

HALIFAXIENSE

The Gorsebrook campus

In 1943, part of the Gorsebrook Golf Club was purchased. The estate was originally the Halifax home of merchant, privateer and banker Enos Collins (1774–1871), reputedly "the wealthiest man in the Lower Provinces." When it became the Gorsebrook Golf Club, the house served as the 19th hole.

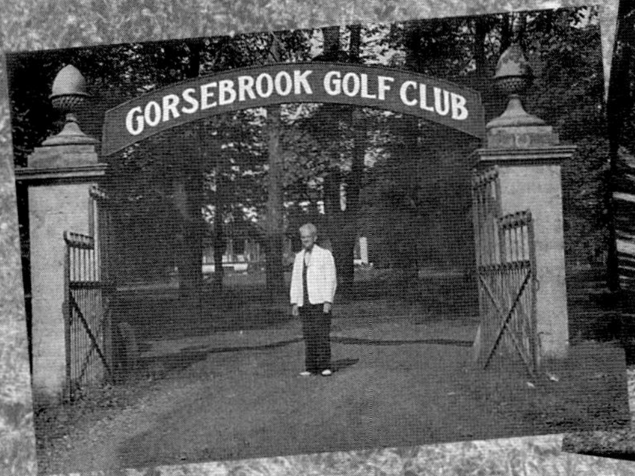

Gorsebrook House, with the McNally building visible in the background. When it was torn down in 1962 to make way for the Student Centre, outrage among local citizens led to the formation of Heritage Trust of Nova Scotia.

Right: The stately gate posts and long stone wall of the Gorsebrook estate still remain on Tower Road.

Far right: One of the fairways.

Action at last

Construction had first to be delayed until the end of the war; then the post-war shortage of steel held it up again.

Below: This sign went up when work began in 1949. Note that the founding date was then considered to be 1841, the date of incorporation.

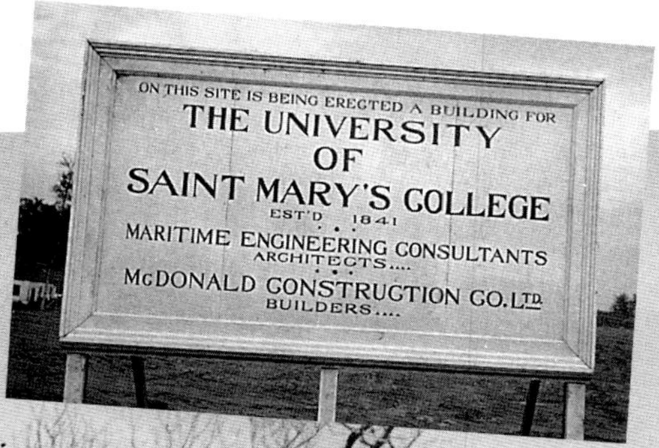

Above: June 24, 1949, Archbishop McNally donned his finest satin and lace and himself turned the sod for construction of the building which bears his name.

Below: The Chapel Choir was on hand to help celebrate the occasion

A new campus – the 1950s

1951 saw the realization of Archbishop McNally's dream—the College and High School moved into the new building. It contained classrooms, student residence rooms and quarters for the Jesuit Fathers. The High School occupied three rooms on the second floor. A year later, the foyer became the home of the new Canadian Martyrs' Parish, established to serve Catholics living in the South End of Halifax and to support the College.

Left: Archbishop McNally makes a tour of inspection. L to R: Father Carroll, SJ, Father Edward Brown, SJ, the Archbishop, B.A. O'Leary, C.P. Flemming.

Below: Stonemasons working on the facade of what is now the McNally Building. The Archbishop built himself an apartment over the main entrance, but it is not known if he ever occupied it.

Below left: The first telephone exchange in the foyer.

Bottom: A residence room 1950s style. The south wing was where the Jesuits lived and in the 1980s many of its offices still had washbasins.

Below right: In 1953, the East Wing of the McNally building opened as the college chapel and Canadian Martyrs' parish church. The gym was located directly under it!

Right: This statue of the University's patron saint still stands in the entrance hall.

More students, more books

The Windsor Street campus contained a modest library. The Robie Street building opened with the E.H. Horne Memorial Library located over its entrance, where the Division of Engineering is today. In 1965 this had to be replaced by the purpose-built Bishop Burke Library. Enrolment continued to mushroom and the much bigger Patrick Power Library opened in 1976.

Right: Working in the library of the Windsor Street Campus under the watchful eye of a Jesuit Father. The calendar shows it was April 1944.

Above right: E.H. Horne Memorial Library. The tables and chairs have survived and are in use in the University Archives.

Women on campus

The 1950s saw battles with Mount Saint Vincent College over whether Saint Mary's should admit women, but the Jesuit Fathers realized that to survive Saint Mary's must become co-educational. In 1953, credit and non-credit evening courses were offered to part-time students, both men and women. In 1954, a non-credit adult studies program began. In 1956, the first women graduated, although the University did not officially become co-educational until 1968.

Top: The first evening credit students, with faculty and staff. L to R, front: Elizabeth Walker, Eileen O'Neil, Alice Bell, Mary MacNeil, Flora McIsaac, n/k. Centre: Anne Walker, n/k, Pearce Currie, Arthur Conrad, n/k, n/k, Jim Britten. Back: n/k, Father W. McCarthy, SJ, Father Art Williams, SJ, Father Daniel O'Rourke, SJ.

Right: Pioneers—convocation 1956 saw the joyful graduation of (L to R) Marion McNutt, Elizabeth Williams, Josephine Mitchell and Carol Mielke. In 2001, slightly more than half of Saint Mary's 7,329 students were women.

The Engineers' Ball

Engineering, first introduced by the Irish Christian Brothers in 1916, was a three-year program. Its students were a lively bunch. Their Annual Ball was a highlight of the social calendar, and they also hosted a rich and varied Talent Show.

Dressed to kill at the February 1955 Engineers' Ball. Remember those Dorothy bags? L to R: Ted Riordon, Margaret Martin, n/k, Doane Hallett (now Justice)

Right: Provincial Premier Robert L. Stanfield speaks at the Engineers' Ball in 1955. L to R: Mrs. Margaret Ryan, wife of Dean of Engineering James L. Ryan, Father Patrick Malone, SJ, Premier Stanfield, Bernard Sheehan, Father Frederick Lynch, SJ (President)

Below: A musical interlude at the Ball, L to R: William Reid, n/k, Bernard Sheehan, Nancy O'Hearn, later Mrs. Sheehan

Homage to Mount Saint Vincent

Despite the distance between the two institutions, Cupid worked hard. There were numerous meeting places around town, some "posh" like the Cameo Café on Spring Garden Road and others less so. Dates for dances were usually "Mounties" and many dynastic marriages were made this way.

A Roman Catholic college

Saint Mary's continued to play a major role in the life of the Roman Catholic church.

Above: Former Saint Mary's students studying at Holy Heart Seminary on Quinpool Road. Probably mid-1940s.

Below: September 22, 1957, saw thousands flocking to the campus for a Demonstration of Faith and Holy Name Parade.

Left: In January 1955, the University received a visit from Papal Delegate Idebrando Antoniutti. L to R: Father Lynch, SJ (President), Ron (Moose) Leblanc, Papal Delegate

Above: Knights of Columbus flank an altar set up on the steps of McNally for the 1955 Demonstration of Faith.

Right: The executive of Sodales, a religious group dedicated to the Virgin Mary. L to R: n/k, Colin Campbell (now Bishop), n/k, and Peter Heenan

The 1960s – expansion!

In the 1960s, tradition collided with the future and sparks flew. Higher education boomed in an era of radical change in morals, dress, music and more. With growing enrolment (547 in 1959 and 2,654 in 1969), it was obvious that Archbishop McNally's white elephant could no longer contain the burgeoning student population. An expansion plan was created and work started. For over a decade, the campus was one huge building site.

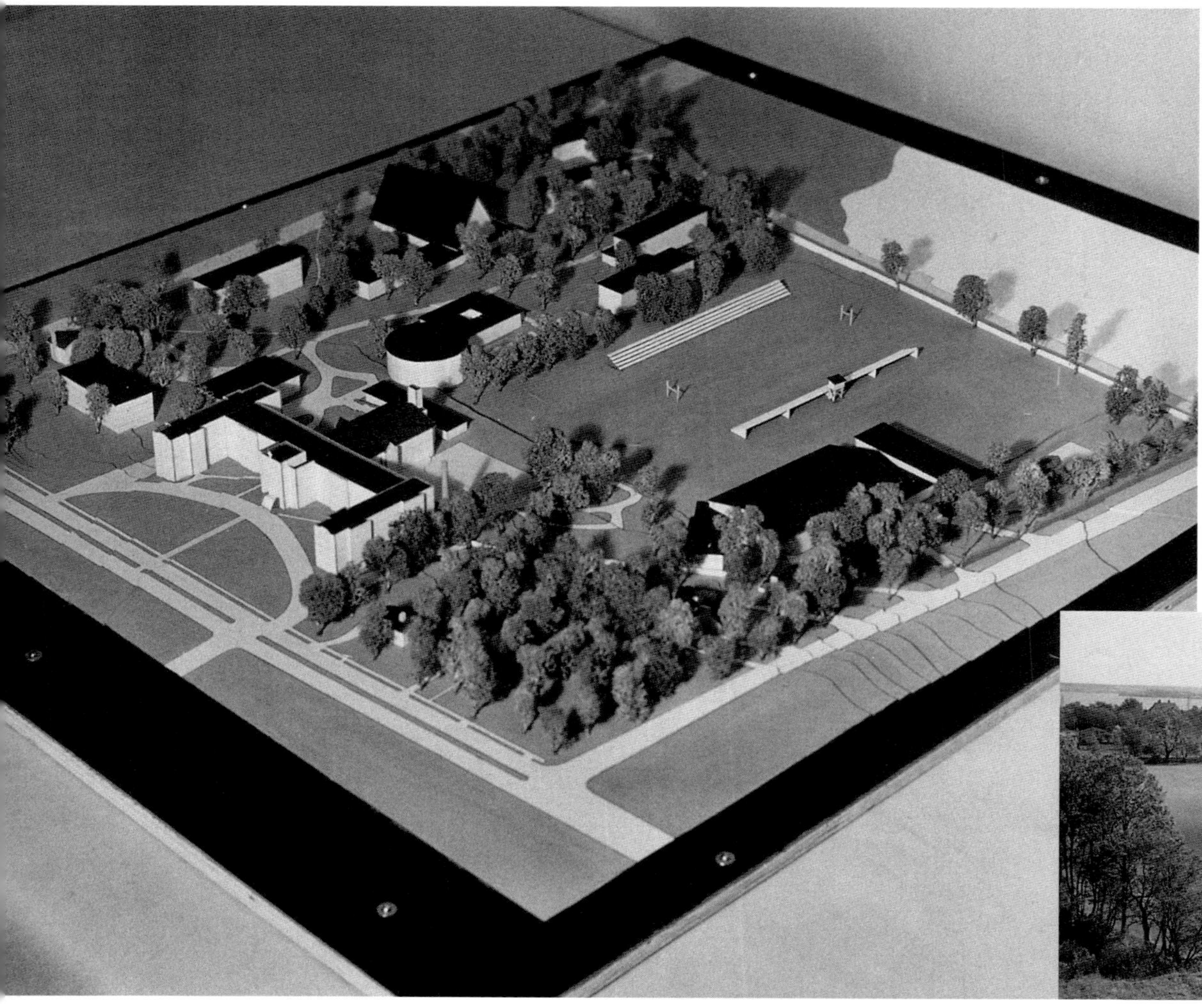

Above: An aerial view of the new campus in its early days, before the pointed spire was added to the chapel.

Left: An early model of the proposed expansion. The Student Centre is a circle rather than the cruciform structure it actually became.

Below: View across an empty expanse of campus to the harbour and McNabs Island

Opposite page:
Background: The Science Building, before construction of the Patrick Power Library. Wherever possible, the buildings were carefully woven together so that students could avoid going outside in winter.

Left: The Bishop Burke Library

Right: The O'Donnell-Hennessey Student Centre, named for two of the Jesuit Fathers

Construction

Collins House was torn down in 1962 to make way for the Student Centre. In 1965, the first library opened and in 1967 the Science Building was complete. 1968 saw the opening of the Rice and Vanier residences. These were not neo-classical buildings in the Ivy League tradition, but modern structures symbolic of an institution reaching to the future. Looked at in 2002, their design has stood the test of time. Huskies Stadium was built in 1969 for the Canada Summer Games.

The living is easy

In 1968, the Rice and Vanier residences opened, offering up-to-date accommodation to students. They had a grocery store, pool, barber shop, beauty salon and four floors specially equipped for students with disabilities. In the beginning, Rice was a men's residence and Vanier was for women only.

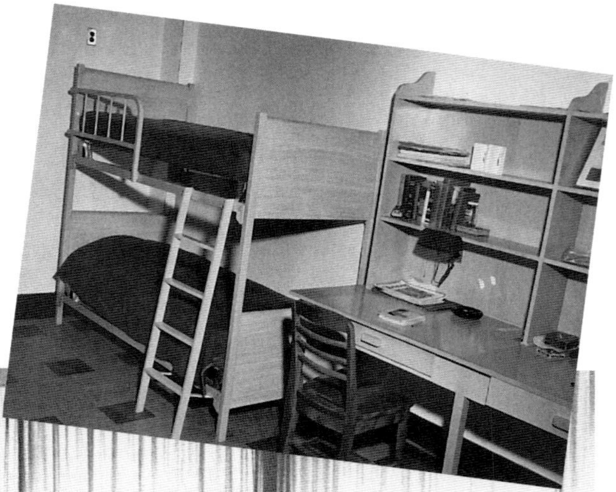

Right: A residence room, 1960s style

Below: The dining area

The campus complete with the Rice and Vanier residences and Huskies Stadium

Changing times

But it wasn't all construction. The 1960s were the years of protest and Saint Mary's saw its share. Music was alive and well and Anne Murray was often on campus. In 1963, the High School closed down with 25 in the final graduating class and in 1968 the University officially became co-educational. During this decade the University moved slowly but surely towards autonomy from the Archdiocese and the appointment of secular faculty and staff.

Left: Anne Murray performs with Bill Langstroth on campus. Many other now-famous musicians were part of the music scene.

Top: Some things never change!

Above: By the end of the decade, a certain relaxation in standards is visible through illustrations in the 1970 Year Book.

The protest years

Students believed they could change the world and protests were the norm. Dress became informal and blue denim arrived—the collar-and-tie days were over.

A protest downtown

The main corridor in McNally under siege

What were the firemen doing?

The Catholic tradition remains

The Jesuits built the Saint Ignatius Chapel on the main floor of the Loyola Academic Complex, right opposite what is now bustling Tim Horton's.

In 2002, it provides an oasis of peace for students of all faiths under the leadership of University Chaplain and Jesuit Father Con Mulvihill.

Crucifix in the chapel

Above: Father Hennessey inhabited a residence apartment for a number of years after retirement, acting as unofficial priest in residence. He is seen here enjoying sun and conversation on the steps of McNally.

Left: At the Christmas party in 1971, Father Stewart (Saint Nick) gives gifts to the cast of the Nativity play.

Athletics: The Jesuit Years

Athletic prowess continues: the 1940s

The Jesuit Fathers continued to build on Saint Mary's reputation for sporting achievement. The teams, like those of most Roman Catholic institutions, were known as the Saints. And once a Saint, always a Saint. The players of yesterday became the coaches and supporters of today—a tradition which still lives.

Above: Frank Baldwin and Father John Power, SJ, flank this high school basketball team from the 1950s. Frank Baldwin was inducted into Saint Mary's University Sport Hall of Fame in 1997.

Left: The legendary Frank Baldwin, Number 11, front row, poses with team mates for the annual team photo. The team represented Saint Mary's College circa 1945.

Previous page: Considered one of the great lines of all time in the history of Nova Scotia junior hockey, Hughie Campbell, Bert Hirschfeld and Elmer MacGillivray brought fame and distinction to the Saint Mary's College hockey program in the late 1940s. Elmer MacGillivray was inducted into the Saint Mary's Sport Hall of Fame in October 2001.

Canadian-style football was on campus in the 1940s. The game was introduced to Halifax by Saint Mary's and Dalhousie in an epic game in 1933. It quickly gained popularity and eventually replaced rugby.

Moving to Robie Street didn't slow them down: the 1950s

Above: A Saint Mary's High School football team, early 1950s, assembled for a team photo behind the Robie Street Building on an area where the Huskies Stadium sits today. This is documented proof that there was football on the campus BH—*Before Hayes*.

Football

Below: In 1956 and 1957 the Saints were the reigning Maritime Junior Football champions. Note the candy-striped uniforms, in vogue in that era.

Hockey

Right: Four hockey players, wearing the Saint Mary's High School hockey uniforms of the 1950s, share a laugh and discuss strategy prior to a big game. They were all "big games" in those years.

Above: Saint Mary's College Hockey team with Father Buck O'Donnell, far right, back row. Note the combination of various sweater types sported in these leaner years. Father O'Donnell was inducted into Saint Mary's University Sport Hall of Fame in 1996.

Below: Saint Mary's Hockey Team of the late 1950s with coach Dugger McNeil, back row left. Can you find Granville Kelly, Jim O'Regan, Jim Warner, Sam Almolky, Bill Conrad, Bill Bailey, Ken Mantin and Ducky Reardon? Or help us name the rest?

The Hayes era begins

In 1958, Elmer MacGillivray, by then a Jesuit priest, recruited Shearwater Flyers' football star, Bob Hayes as the new athletic director. Although they were still the "Jesuit Years," the arrival of Bob Hayes meant the beginning of something very special—the Hayes era. Legends about Bob could fill an entire book and, in 2001, he was appointed *Athletic Director Emeritus.* Does any other university have one of these rare birds?

Above: Bob Hayes as successful player

Above right: Bob Hayes (second left, back row) coached the Huskies to the Atlantic Bowl championship in 1964, laying the foundation for a football program most consider to be a model for universities across Canada.

Right: Can you name these Saint Mary's gridironers? The team played in the 1960s.

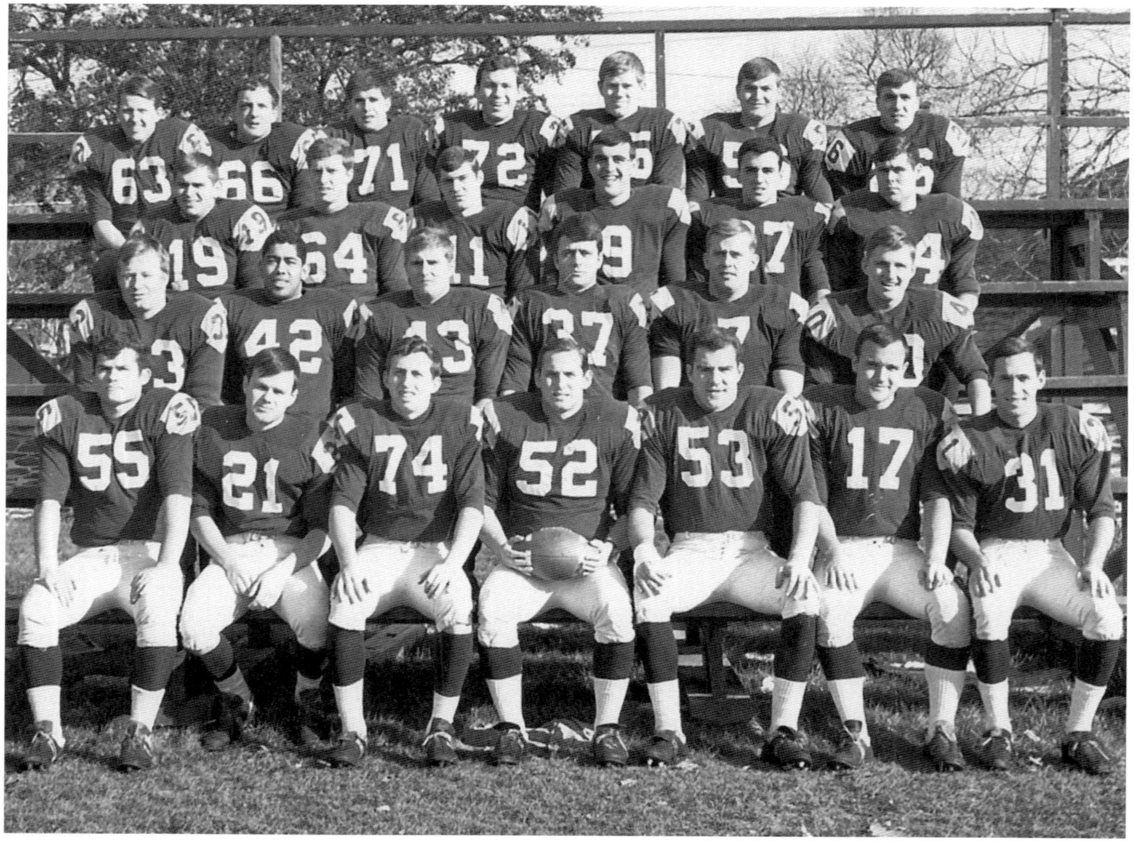

Basketball

Coach Les Goodwin ran up an impressive record during the 1960s. He and Frank Baldwin are credited with the foundation of what has become a national force in basketball.

Above: Bob Lahey (R) receives an award from Coach Goodwin. In 1996, Lahey, a Saint Mary's sporting legend, was the first player to be inducted into the Saint Mary's University Sport Hall of Fame.

Below: A 1960s edition of the Saint Mary's Basketball Huskies with (front row, L to R) Team Manager Dick MacLean, Coach Les Goodwin, Father J.J. Hennessey, SJ, n/k. In 1955, the much loved and revered Father Hennessey and Bob Hayes were the first inductees into the Saint Mary's University Sport Hall of Fame.

Bill Mullane goes high to the net in this action shot taken circa 1960.

Huskies beat out Belted Kingfishers

Until 1960, Saint Mary's Saints reigned. During that year, an article appeared in the *Journal* explaining the need for a mascot for the athletic teams at the University. A grand total of two people offered their ideas and, had the Committee let the matter end with this input, our teams would have been the "Belted Kingfishers." After adopting the name, that of the bird which was on the crest of the City of Halifax, sober second thought had the motion withdrawn and eventually the name Huskies was chosen.

Kimo, one of two Husky dogs who served as the official mascot for Huskies teams. In later years, they were replaced by students in furry costumes, who proved easier to handle.

Keith Hotchkiss and Bob Hayes show off new SMU clothing at the bookstore, probably in the early 1970s. Keith, one of the winning 1973 Football Huskies, is Director of Student Services.

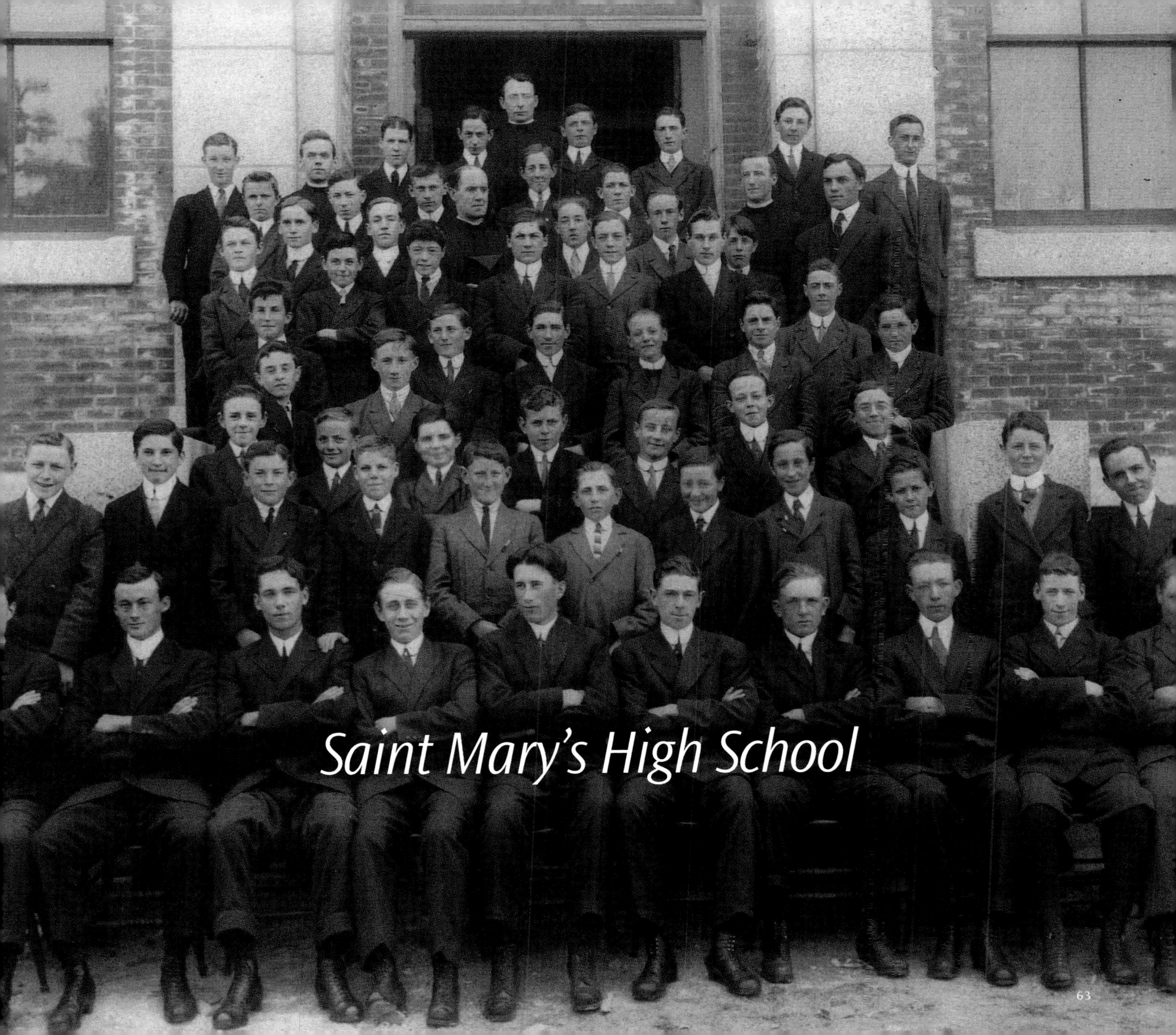

Saint Mary's High School

Saint Mary's High School

The Archdiocese of Halifax operated a secondary school for boys sporadically from the mid-1800s. When Archbishop O'Brien re-opened Saint Mary's in 1903, it was a two-year pre-college institution. When degree courses were reinstated by the Irish Christian Brothers in 1913, the High School and College shared the Windsor Street campus. The running of both institutions was taken over by the Jesuits in 1940. Over the years, the High School educated some 2,000 young Catholics.

Previous page: Saint Mary's High School class photo, 1913–1914

Right: Notman Studio photograph of building on Barrington Street, next to the Glebe House, built for Saint Mary's Boys' School in 1864 for $16,000

Below: The first-year class, in 1917–18

Hockey disappointment

In 1933, Brother Garvey's carefully picked and trained High School teams did well. The Junior team, which contained almost the same players as the Senior, beat Chester in the first of two games in the semi-final of the Provincial championship.

Warm weather delayed the second game. Lent, with its ban on competitive sport, began and Saint Mary's had to concede. Team member Bruce Flemming told his son David (High School '62) that Brother Garvey's faith was severely tested.

Above: Sport was an important part of education. The young hopefuls of the 1943 Junior High hockey team were: L to R, Front: K. O'Toole, M. Murphy, J. Gordon, A. Keith, M. Chouinard. Back: E. Drysdale, D. Drillio, A. Forter, W. Perron and M. Fougere.

The 1933 Junior-Senior High School Hockey Team. L to R: Frank Charlton, John Mullane, Bruce Flemming, Roy Edgar, Everett Ennis, John Dickie, Dough Chisholm, Frank Foley, John "Buzz" Bulley, James Lovett.

Drama and dancing

Left: High School pupils learned Scottish dancing.

... and the kilts came in handy for drama—could this be Macbeth?

The new campus

In 1951, the High School moved with Saint Mary's College to the Robie Street campus, where it occupied three rooms on the second floor of the new building.

Above: RAC cadets work on their morse code.

Below: High School students pose in the entrance hall of the new building.

The end

Saint Mary's High School closed in 1963.

Right: The penultimate class as grade 10 students in 1961. L to R, back: Pat Brownlow, David Flemming, Wayne Hollett, Barry Hart, Ron Jollemore, Greg Tanner, Kent Robinson, Denis Cassivi, Paul Giroux, John Wade, John MacDonald, Wayne Bennett, Ken Spencer. Middle: Father John Lesage, Andy Carey, Bruce Halliday, Jim Landry, Mike MacGillivray, James O'Hagen, Paul Vorstermans, Roger Flinn, Bob Smith, John Lawlor, Donnie Brown, René McKinnon, John Delaney, Ian Stewart. Front: Mike Dempster, Tom Delvallet, Murdoch Reteff, Bob Mackasey, Chris Donahoe, Fred MacGillivray, Helmut Hanelein, David Eagen, Greg Carruthers, Carey McFeters.

The reunion

In May,1988, a 25-year reunion was held for alumni of the High School. In the program alumnus Guy Pothier said: "The school thought it knew what its students should know. And its certainty, its confidence in its mission, resting ultimately of course on religious conviction, gave it an undeniable authority and appeal, whatever reservations one might have had then or later."

Some of the organizers: clockwise from bottom: David Flemming, Tom Goodyear, Pat Curran, Terry Coughlan, John Delaney, Guy Pothier, Fred MacGillivray

Left: Alumni at the reunion. Front and centre, Father William Stewart, SJ

A Public University

Early in 1970, the wheels were set in motion for an orderly transition of the ownership and administration of Saint Mary's to a 30-member board of governors. The University's assets were transferred and *An Act to Amend and Consolidate the Acts Relating to Saint Mary's University* was passed by the Government of Nova Scotia. Relations between the University and the Archdiocese remained cordial and the University maintained its Roman Catholic traditions. The Archbishop continued to serve as Chancellor. Edmund Morris, a Roman Catholic layman and High School graduate, served as interim president for one year.

The first meeting of the new board, July 31, 1970:
Above left: Rev. James Hayes, Archbishop and Chancellor

Above right: Board Chairman Austin Burke and the University seal

Right (L to R): Rev. Colin Campbell, Rev. James Hayes, Interim President Edmund Morris

Expansion continues

The ambitious expansion plan of the 1960s was completed with the opening of the Loyola Academic and Residence Complex in 1971 and a new Canadian Martyrs' Church in the same year.

Right: President Edmund Morris (centre) continues the building inspection tradition as he checks out the new Loyola building.

Inset: Loyola under construction

Below: This 1970 cartoon by Bob Chambers in the *Halifax Herald* shows rivalry between Saint Mary's President Edmund Morris and Dalhousie President Henry Hicks.

The second tower

Loyola: a fine new academic and residence complex, complete with married students' quarters. Thirty years later, a complete makeover has installed internet connections in all apartments.

Above: Students soon left their mark on the tunnel between Loyola and Vanier.

Right: Moving into Rice, with Loyola in the background

A new Canadian Martyrs' Church

1971 saw the opening of a new church for Canadian Martyrs' parish. It continued to be closely connected with the University, playing the role of chapel whenever needed.

Canadian Martyrs' Church, Inglis Street

Construction of the new church allowed the old chapel to be used first as a reading room and later as the Theatre Auditorium.

Dr. Owen Carrigan

In 1971, Dr. Owen Carrigan became president and, until 1979, watched over the steady transformation of the University into a modern institution. He was instrumental in bringing another new library to campus and focused particularly on raising faculty qualifications: in 2001, 92.4 per cent of Saint Mary's faculty had PhDs, the second highest in Canada for primarily undergraduate universities. In 1974, a faculty union was certified.

Left: Despite some turbulent early years, remarkably good relations have prevailed between faculty and the University since 1974. No strike has ever taken place. Dalhousie faculty sought "Parity with St. Mary's" when they struck in 1998 and again in 2002.

Below: Convocation in the Old Chapel during the Carrigan years, 1976

Dr. Carrigan presents a medal at Convocation 1972.

Another new library

The 1965 Burke library proved unequal to the needs of the rising student population and in 1976 the Patrick Power Library opened.

Above: Staff of the Patrick Power Library in the fall of 1990

Left: The Patrick Power Library, named for the University's 1881 benefactor

Below: Before construction could begin, alterations had to be made to the South wing of McNally.

A great place to study

Celebration: The 175th Anniversary

In 1977, the University celebrated 175 years from Bishop Edmund Burke's first efforts to provide an education for Roman Catholic youth.

A mass was held in the old chapel.

Staff and faculty danced
and dined the night away.

The Ozmon years – 1979 to 2000

Under Dr. Kenneth Ozmon Saint Mary's achieved growth and stability. There were 2,654 full- and part-time students when he was installed and over 7,000 when he retired 21 years later. His term, which he describes as a team effort, was characterized by academic and international growth and by putting the needs of students first. The Quality of Teaching Committee was introduced to help faculty hone their classroom skills.

In 1990, campus culture was changed forever by the arrival of Tim Horton's super-caffeine shots and mouth-watering donuts. In this picture Dr. Ozmon serves coffee as part of a fundraiser for a childrens' charity.

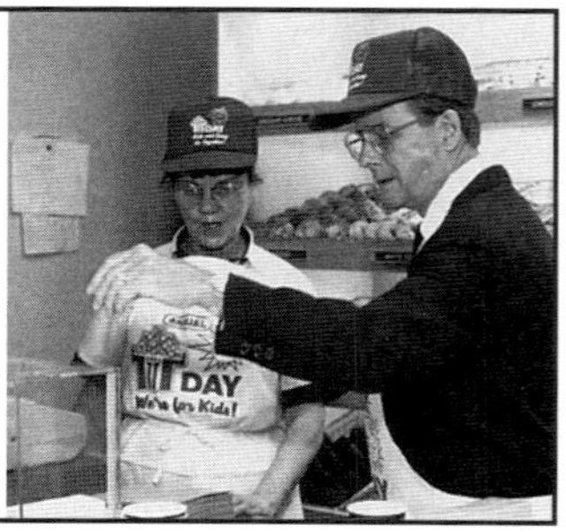

Left: The installation of Dr. Kenneth L. Ozmon in 1979. L to R: Dr. Ozmon, Dr. Peter Meincke (President, University of P.E.I., where Dr. Ozmon had been Dean of Arts), Bishop Colin Campbell (Chancellor)

Below: Elizabeth Ozmon was a hard working Mrs. Pres. who became involved in many aspects of campus life.

New academic programs

Academic innovations by the public university included the Institute of Human Values and a Criminology Certificate (1975), the International Education Centre (1979), Co-op Education, Asian Studies and the China Program, the Gorsebrook Institute for Atlantic Canada Studies (1982), the D'Arcy McGee Chair of Irish Studies (1986) and the Atlantic Centre for Environmental Studies (1992).

Above: Dr. Mary Sun with a group of students enrolled in the Asian Studies Program.

Studying our Irish roots

Saint Mary's Irish roots have never been forgotten. In the days of the Irish Christian Brothers, a medal was awarded for Irish History. Since joining the English Department in 1970, Dr. Cyril Byrne, OC, has worked tirelessly to encourage these studies. His efforts resulted in the foundation of the D'Arcy McGee Chair of Irish Studies in 1986.

1996, graduation of the first Irish Studies major. L to R: Pádraig Ó Siadhail (Chair of Irish Studies), Pauline Hingston BA, Dr. Cyril Byrne (Co-ordinator, Irish Studies Program)

Below: Donal Begley, the Chief Herald of Ireland (L) presented Dr. Ozmon with a coat of arms for the D'Arcy McGee Chair of Irish Studies in 1987.

Below right: A valuable facsimile of the Book of Kells, presented to the University by the Charitable Irish Society in 1990

Pan-Am Games, 1982

Hosting the Pan-Am Wheelchair Games in 1982 brought the artificial turf field and running track to campus.

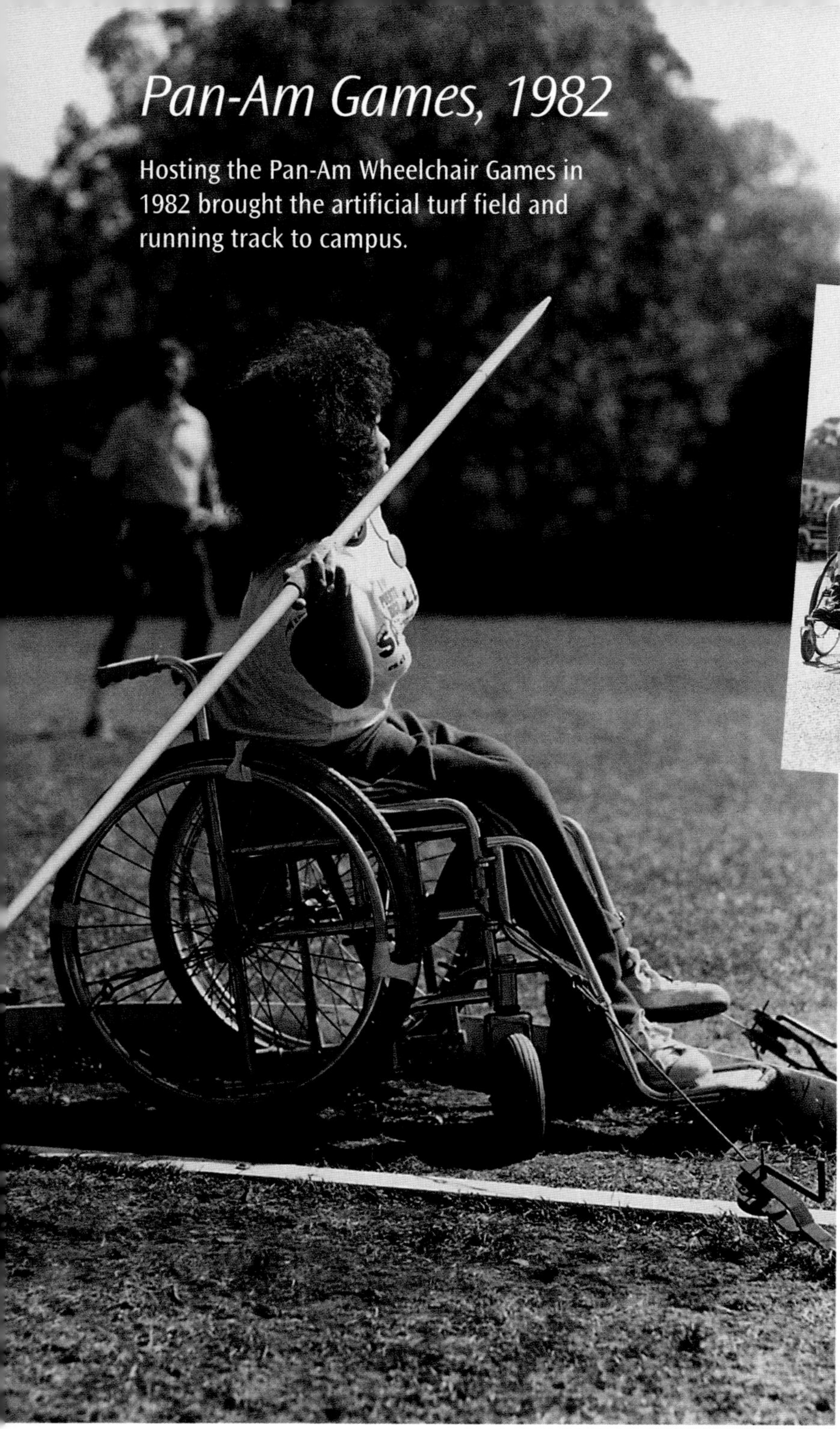

Left and below: Athletes perform at the Pan-Am Games.

Below: Rick Hansen was a medal winner at the Pan-Am games.

Bottom left: Turning the sod for the new field. L to R: Ken MacRae, n/k, Gerald Regan (Minister for Fitness and Amateur Sport) and Dr. Ozmon

Bottom right: Lighting the flame at the Pan-Am Games

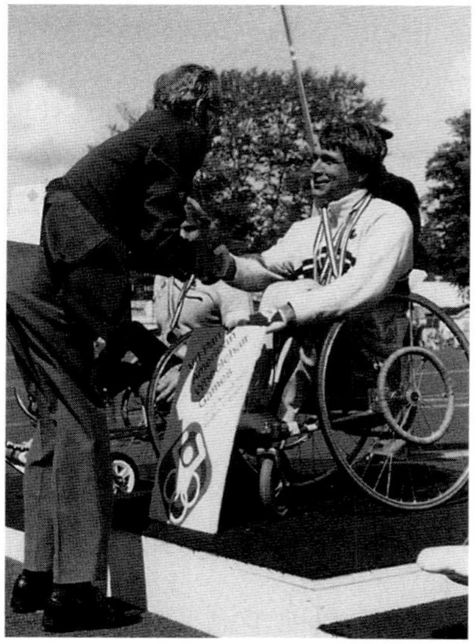

Students with disabilities

In 1985 the University's long-standing concern for students with disabilities resulted in the opening of the Atlantic Centre of Research, Access and Support for Students with Disabilities.

Right: Archbishop James Hayes congratulates Martin Gill at Convocation 1985.

Centre: Well known man-about-campus Donny Jackson

Below: Cutting the ribbon. L to R: Dr. Ozmon, Edmund Morris (then N.S. Minister of Social Services), Stewart McInnes (Federal Minister of Public Works), Tom McInnis (N.S. Education Minister), David Leitch (Director, Atlantic Centre)

The Tower opens

The 1987 opening of The Tower added a first-class sports facility to campus—a facility which is open to all Haligonians.

Below left: The Tower takes shape

Below right: In September 1985, sod was turned for The Tower by (L to R) N.S. Attorney General (and alumnus) Terry Donahoe, University painter Vern Creighton and N.S. Premier John Buchanan. The same cast of characters cut the ribbon to open the facility on September 19, 1987.

The site is laid out for construction.

The Tower

Ingenuity makes space

The Old Gym, scene of many legendary sporting battles, came vacant when The Tower opened. Imaginative use of this space produced two floors of classrooms and computer labs and a faculty lounge.

Architect's drawing of the new facilities shoehorned into the Old Gym

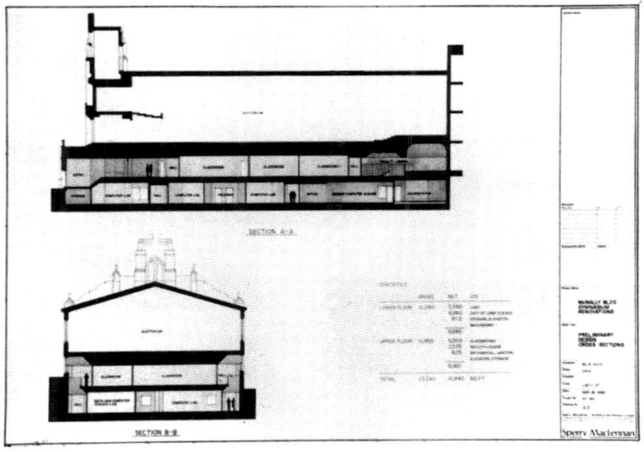

It all takes $$$

Fundraising had by now become a major occupation for the President, dedicated volunteers and development staff. The first capital campaign ran from 1984 to 1989 and raised $14 million. The *Building on Strength* campaign ran from 1994 to 1999 and raised over $24 million. There is also an annual appeal to Saint Mary's huge family of faithful alumni; the 2001 *Maclean's* Universities issue reported that almost 28 per cent of them support their *alma mater*—second among undergraduate universities! Thank you!

Below right, top to bottom: The annual house draw proved popular.

Students helped by working in the call centre.

Saying "Thank-you" to Bill Mingo, who co-chaired the 1984–89 capital campaign with Ronald Downie, QC, and John Dickie, QC. L to R: Elizabeth Ozmon, Bill Mingo, Edith Mingo and Dr. Ozmon.

A tailgate party in the Tower parking lot launched the 1994 *Building on Strength* campaign. Behind the grill were volunteers (L to R) Suzanne Sheaves (Campaign Cabinet), Martha Jodrey (Kick-off Event Chair), Denis Ryan (Event MC), Ted Flinn (Chairman of the Board), David Sobey (Campaign Chair).

Left: Don Keleher was Frosh of the Year in 1966. In 2001, this engineering grad turned Development Director retired after 20 years of service to Saint Mary's.

Below: Kicking off the local corporate section of the 1984–89 Capital Campaign. L to R: Development Director Don Keleher, Chair Bob Shaw, and Dr Ozmon.

Saint Mary's students – an amazing bunch

Picking a few students from the galaxy of stars who have passed through the University is a recipe for disaster. But these students will give a feeling for the remarkable young people for whom Saint Mary's is a springboard to the future.

Clockwise from left:

Canada Scholarship winners in 1991

David Sykes, Saint Mary's quarterback and 1994 Rhodes Scholar, with Professor Edward McBride (Political Science)

In 1988, these SMU graduates were studying at Dalhousie law school.

Environmental activist Thea Wilson-Hammond, 1992

Some of SMU's outstanding math students with APICS trophy in 1999/2000

Student leaders

Top: Student President Sanjeev Chowdhury with John Bishop and Loretta Smith at a reception for graduates of 1989. In 2002, Sanjeev is press secretary to Deputy PM John Manley.

Bottom: Incoming student president Carrie Schurr (L) watches as President Mark Bower presents Kaye O'Keefe with a Gold M award for her service to students during 20 years at Saint Mary's (1987).

Rationalization

It didn't work in the 1870s and it didn't work in the 1920s, but in the late 1980s and early 1990s, the government of Nova Scotia tried to amalgamate some of the 11 degree-granting institutions in the province. Several years of negotiations were unable to overcome the reluctance of these universities to sink their very real cultural and historic differences in one or more merged institutions. Apart from the closure of the N.S. Teachers' College and several teacher training programs (including Saint Mary's), and the absorption of TUNS by Dalhousie, the *status quo* remains. However, many examples of co-operation resulted from the process and in 1996, seven universities formed the Metro Consortium to encourage resource sharing.

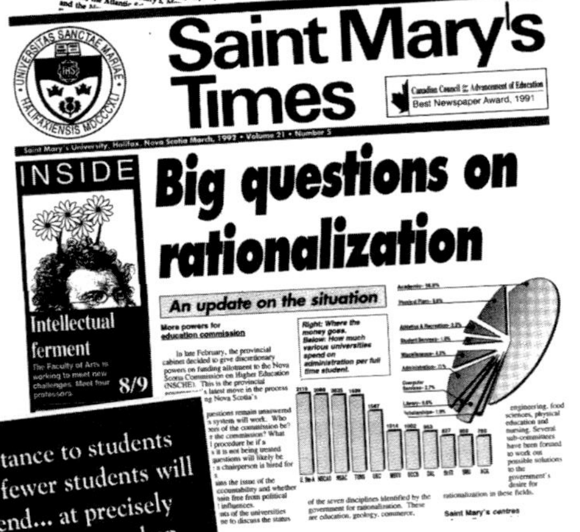

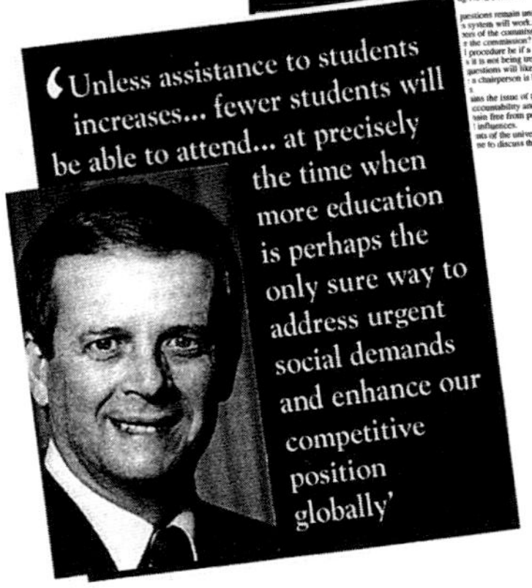

The future of Saint Mary's

In 1989, The President's Committee on the Future of the University, chaired by former Brock University President Dr. Alan Earp, began deliberating on how to cope with the results of rapid expansion. L to R: Fred Crooks, Dr. Donald Weeren, Dr. Grace Pretty, Dr. Hermann Schwind, Dr. Kenneth Ozmon, Dr. Alan Earp, Diana Lidstone, Dr. Wendy Katz, Dr. Stephen Davis, Margaret Ann Bennett.

Top: In 1995, Saint Mary's *Journal* reported the creation of a co-operative partnership between Mount Saint Vincent, the Nova Scotia College of Art and Design, the Atlantic School of Theology and Saint Mary's, which could save $4 million a year.

Middle: Front page news in March 1992, *Saint Mary's Times*

Bottom: Dr. Ozmon chaired the Metro Universities Presidents' Committee during these tough years. He expressed his views on rationalization in this 1991 *Halifax Herald* article which was reproduced in Saint Mary's *Times.*

The global stage

The 1990s saw much globe trotting by administration and faculty of Saint Mary's as it became part of Canada's foreign aid initiative and embraced the concept of globalization. The University reached out to take education to the developing nations and also created educational partnerships with developed countries. China, Japan, Mexico, the Caribbean, Iceland, you name it, a link was forged. After the breakup of the USSR, Saint Mary's moved to help teach its former members how to introduce market-based economies.

Gambia convocation

A relationship with The Gambia, begun in 1993, saw many faculty and staff spending whole semesters in that country, providing undergraduate education for its young people. The long-term goal is to establish the University of The Gambia. In 1999, a team from Saint Mary's went to The Gambia to award 62 degrees at a SMU convocation.

Top: Dean of Arts Mike Larsen with one of the graduates

Above: Music for convocation

Right: Dr. and Mrs. Ozman and the president of The Gambia pose with the graduates.

A new home for Commerce

1n 1998, the state-of-the-art Frank H. Sobey Building, named for the legendary grocer, opened as the new home of the Faculty of Commerce, which also bears his name.

An early discussion on building possibilities. L to R: Joseph Richards (Commerce Soc.), Dr. Cathy Driscoll, Dr. David Gray, Dr. Colin Dodds (V-P Academic), Dr. Paul Dixon (Dean of Commerce)

Right: Nova Scotia Premier John Savage turned the sod 1990s-style, watched by Board Chairman Jack Keith and Dr. Ozmon.

Right: Opening day: a proud moment for Guy Nöel (R), V-P. Administration, seen here with board member Michael Zatzman

Frank H. Sobey, founder of the Stellarton, N.S., grocery empire

David Sobey, long time Board of Governors member and hard working chair of the *Building on Strength* campaign, which made the new building possible

Revamping the residences

In the early 1990s, the 30-year-old residence towers began to show their age. In the winter of 1994, residents of Rice and Vanier had to be evacuated to downtown hotels while major repairs were undertaken. Over the 2000–01 academic year, the Loyola residence was completely renovated and equipped with state-of-the-art communication technology. On this occasion, the students were housed in a high rise behind the former Halifax Infirmary.

The Rice Residence under re-construction

Cutting the ribbon to reopen the Loyola residence, September 2001. Doing the honours, Samantha Anderson (SMUSA Pres.), Jane Purves (NS Minister of Education), Chancellor Most Rev. Terrence Prendergast and President Colin Dodds

A new millennium

Saint Mary's began the new millennium with a new president, former Dean of Commerce and Academic Vice-President Dr. Colin Dodds, its first PhD program and over 7,000 full- and part-time students. Making life better for students remained a focus and September 2000 saw the opening of a Centre for New Students. As the bicentennial year begins, planning is in hand for a major capital campaign to improve facilities and continue the revitalization of older buildings.

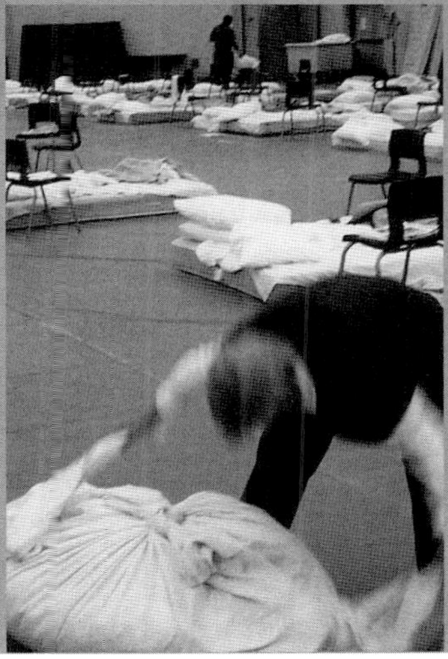

Above: On September 11, 2001, The Tower became home to the crew and passengers of a British Airways flight stranded in Halifax by the New York disaster. In this picture, staff are clearing up.

Left: Dr. Colin Dodds receives his induction medal on October 22, 2000.

Below: Summer 2000 saw the first candidate enrolled in Saint Mary's PhD program in Business Administration-Management, the first such program in Atlantic Canada.

Above: Dr. Helen Ralston pours at "Time for Tea," a fundraiser for a bursary for a single-parent student, hosted by Carol Dodds, wife of the new president, in June 2001.

Left: Director of Admissions Greg Ferguson with new student Adam Dennis and staff Amy Smith and Heather Maxwell

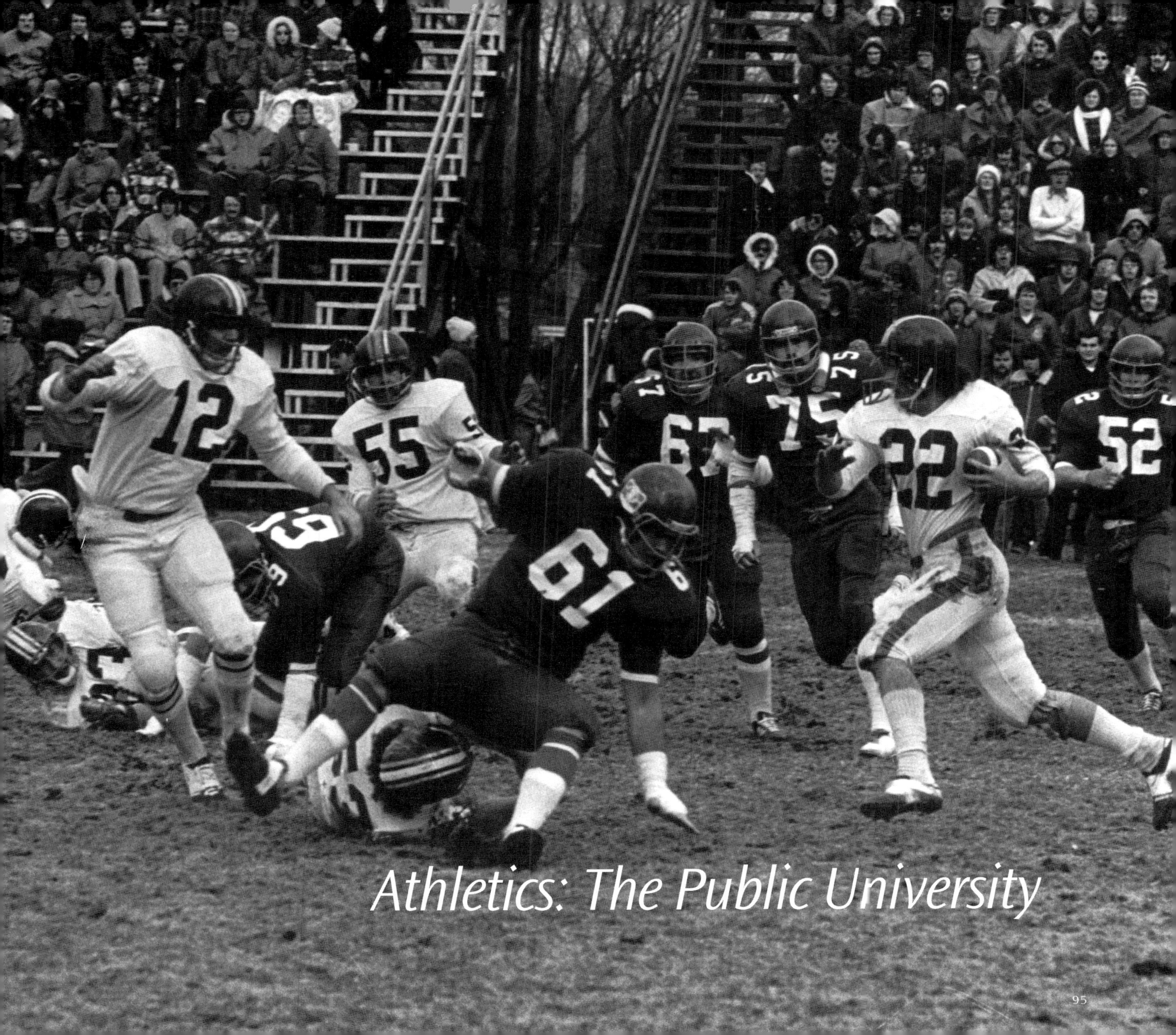

Athletics: The Public University

Athletics: The winning Huskies

Saint Mary's reputation as a football powerhouse rose to new heights in 1973 when the team brought home the Vanier Cup.

Previous page: Action in the 1973 Atlantic Bowl, leading up to the great victory. Note the mud they played on.

Below: Champions all: Coach Keith and his national champions of 1973

Below: It's dinner at the Derby after the big win. Coach Al Keith (third from left) took the football Huskies to the Derby for one of their famous Derby-style steaks. L to R, back: Jimmy Rodger, Hector Poitier; Front: Steve Telfer, Al Keith, Ken Clark

Above: Hair! Hair! Angelo Santucci, who was inducted into SMU's Sport Hall of Fame in October 2001, was a key player on the 1973 championship team. Angelo, who later got a haircut, went on to be an all-star player in the CFL.

Right: Got a light? Things were not so politically correct in days of yore. Here fan Vince McSweeney talks with Ken Clark during the 1973 Vanier Cup game, played at CNE Stadium in Toronto. At the time of the 20-year reunion, Ken, who played in four professional leagues, was kicker for the Ottawa Roughriders.

Below: The 1973 Vanier Cup winners held a reunion in 1993 to mark the 20th anniversary of bringing SMU its first national football title.

Women on court and field

It didn't take long for the female Huskies to make their mark under the leadership of Kathy Mullane. She joined Saint Mary's in 1973 as its basketball coach and director of women's athletics and led her teams to four AUAA titles. Today she is Manager of Facilities and Programming and was inducted into the Sports Hall of Fame in October 2000.

Below: The 1977–78 Women's Field Hockey team (Kathy Mullane left), were AUAA champs and placed third in CIAU.

Right: The Women's Field Hockey Huskies in action

Left: The Huskies' Lisa Johnson (L) close checking a St. Francis Xavier player in a 1986 game

Above: Erin O'Brien battles a UNB player for the ball during the 1994 championship game. The Huskies lost this one 2–0.

Above: In 1988–89, Saint Mary's captured the AUAA Field Hockey Championship. Coach Jill Jeffrey, back right

Basketball

Left: Women's basketball. A SMU forward goes by an "X" defender in an AUAA contest in the 1990s.

Above: SMU rookie Jad Crnogorac dribbles down court at the 1994 first annual Cantel Huskies invitational women's basketball tournament at The Tower.

Soccer

Right: Using her head. Players battle away in action in a women's AUAA soccer game.

Far right: SMU Keeper Shelly Whitman was hailed as a vital part of a Huskies team preparing to repeat as AUAA Women's Soccer champions in 1993.

Below: Suzanne Muir (R) battles a Dalhousie Tiger for a loose ball during AUAA playoff action in 1992.

Below: Women's soccer action at Huskies Stadium in a game played in the 1991 season

There's more to sport than CIAU battles

Sporting activities at Saint Mary's have been many and various over the years. A few of them are captured here.

Above left: Rugby made an occasional comeback.

Above centre: Intramural volleyball players give the "we're number one" sign and show off a trophy they won.

Above : A smartly attired cricket team

Left: When tuna fishing was a sport...Yale, Harvard, Dartmouth, Princeton, Toronto, Western, Dalhousie, St. F.X. and SMU took part in the three-day event held in the waters off Yarmouth. This 1975 team was coached by Edmund Morris and Walter Fitzgerald. The event combined sport fishing with a marine biology seminar!

Right: Meet your 1977 golf team.

Above: In the early 1980s, heavy rain and a quick freeze turned Huskies Stadium turf into a giant skating rink.

Above: Tennis anyone? Students relax in a game of tennis after a long day in the classroom.

Basketball

Many fine players have worn the Basketball Huskies' maroon and white, and Brian Heaney and Ross Quackenbush are among their outstanding coaches.

Right: CIAU Basketball Champions 1973. Front row, left to right: Mickey Fox, Lars Gaudguer, John Gallinaugh, Peter Halpin, Bob Taboski, and Lee Thomas. Back row, left to right: John Landry, Brian Burgess, Art Watters, Otha Johnson, Fred Perry, Greig Redding and Coach Brian Heaney

Left: Ron "The Hawk" McFarlane with Coach Heaney and SMU President Owen Carrigan, lift the CIAU national trophy in a 1978 victory salute.

Left: Coach Brian Heaney and his 1977–78 CIAU National Basketball Champions display their title banner and celebrate a great victory in front of 11,000 fans in the Metro Centre.

Left: Jason Medford (centre), who was Saint Mary's Male Athlete of the Year, made his presence known on the court. Medford, along with two other Huskies players, box in an Acadia Axemen player.

Below: Mickey Fox goes high to the bucket in a game against Concordia in the 1980–81 season.

Above: Saint Mary's is Number One! Huskies take 1999 national title with a 73–69 victory over top seeded Alberta Golden Bears. Pictured here are an emotional Cyril Smith, Paul Bromby, and Ryan McClintock.

Right: John Landry, trainer extraordinaire, reads a letter of congratulations and praise for his long service to SMU sports teams.

Will Njuko gets ready to sink two for his Huskies.

Below: Coach Ross Quackenbush discusses a play with some of his players.

Where would the Huskies be without the fans?

Left: Harriet and Hennessey Huskie, SMU's sled-dogs, paw for a ride to the Toronto Skydome. They were there supporting the 1990 Huskies and their quest for a Vanier Cup.

Right: Huskies Stadium is filled to capacity with students, alumni and supporters of the Huskies.

Below: "West versus Best" said it all as these fans cheer on the Huskies at the Vanier Cup.

Below: Almost too exciting! Fan at the Metro Centre during the 1978 basketbal tourney

Bottom: Huskies fans let the world (the Tower Road portion) know who is Number 1.

Above: "Here we go Huskies, here we go." Vern "The Painter" Creighton, a fixture at SMU sporting events, urges on the fans at Huskies Stadium.

Below: Cheerleaders urge the crowd to get behind the Huskies at a basketball game, played at the Metro Centre.

SMU fan indicates victory is a snap.

Hockey

In the 1970s, Coach Bob Boucher took a struggling program and built a hockey dynasty at SMU. Rated one of the top university coaches in Canada, his presence and the reputation of his teams put SMU at the top of the wish ladder for many budding young hockey stars.

Right: Hockey schools were introduced by Coach Bob Boucher, shown here with Dale Turner, Bob Warner and one of the aspiring Huskies.

Hockey Huskies with Coach Boucher, centre front row

Above: Saint Mary's battles arch-rivals Dalhousie in a 1980s AUAA hockey game.

Below: Going to practice. A SMU player makes his way across campus to the Winter Garden Arena and a practice with Coach Boucher.

Far left: Posing on ice. Four Huskies make pretty for the camera prior to a game at the Winter Gardens Arena.

Left: In 2002, the Hockey Huskies celebrate their win over the Dalhousie Tigers in the Atlantic University Sport (AUS) final game. The AUS champs went on to play in the Canadian Inter-University Sport finals.

Huskies celebrate a goal in a CIAU playoff game against the University of Toronto.

Football

Former Montréal Alouette Larry Uteck's years as Football Huskies Head Coach were marked by great teams and spectacular near misses. Larry went on to become Athletics Director and helped to revitalize the athletic program, making it one of best in Canada. He finally got his Vanier Cup in 2001.

Above: A special moment happened just after the Huskies captured the 2001 Vanier Cup. The players scaled the bleachers, taking the cup to Athletic Director Larry Uteck. Players and coaching staff acknowledge that it was Larry who laid the foundation that made this championship possible.

Left: Chris Flynn, thought by many to be the most outstanding football player to wear the Maroon and White, was the big star from 1987 to 1990. Here he avoids two Acadia tacklers. Chris was inducted into the SMU Sports Hall of Fame in 2001.

Below: Larry Uteck in 1987, as head coach of the football Huskies.

Vanier Cup 2001

Right: In 2001, a jam packed Gorsebrook Lounge was alive with excitement as students, faculty and alumni watched their beloved Huskies defeat the University of Manitoba Bisons to give SMU its first national football title since 1973.

Below: Trained by coach Blake Nill in 2001, Huskies players hoist the Vanier Cup for the first time in 28 years.

Soccer

Coach Roy Clements raised the bar when he arrived at SMU and established a soccer program that was the envy of many rival institutions of learning.

Above: Saint Mary's striker George Kyreakous goes by an Acadia player in a AUAA soccer game played at Huskies Stadium

Left: Soccer on the field before the Astro-Turf was installed

Below: Coach Clements, second from left back row, with one of his soccer powerhouses. Peter Wicha, left back, followed in Coach Clements' footsteps.

Winners all!

Above: Jamie Bone, elected to SMU's Sports Hall of Fame in 1999, is shown here sprinting for the line in Seoul, South Korea.

Below: Malcolm (Mac) Davis, Male Athlete of the Year, congratulates Nancy Collins, Female Athlete of the Year, following the 1978 Annual Awards Banquet.

Part Two

Snapshots of Saint Mary's

The photo essays that follow are reminders of what it felt like to be a student or a faculty or staff member at Saint Mary's. We look at the inexorable progress of the academic year, what happens in the classroom, the lighter side of student life and more.

The Academic Year Unfolds

Registration

Each year some students are starting their academic careers and others are reaching the end, but for everyone the framework is the same. It starts with registration and, for the lucky ones, ends with convocation. In between come a thousand experiences.

In the 1980s and 1990s, registration meant endless waiting—but it was a wonderful way to meet people. However, few would exchange the lineups of yesteryear for today's numerous options, including on-line registration. You can even make those painful payments on-line.

Left: Paying the old-fashioned way, 1970

Above: The long wait!

Right: But the weather is nice.

Opposite page: Registration itself

MODERN LANGUAGES
& CLASSICS

Once Labour Day has passed, the Welcome banner goes up on Inglis Street and Frosh Week begins. In the early 1980s, initiation gave way to milder forms of entertainment designed to encourage new students to mix and mingle.

Above: The Welcome banner on Robie Street, frequently stolen by Dal!

Right: Frosh Week activities,1980s

Below: Life was still tough for engineering students in 1986. Initiation left a trail of mustard, ketchup, chocolate syrup and kitty litter in front of the McNally building.

Right: The President's Dinner for New Students is a welcoming tradition. Dr. Ozmon (L) presided in 1994.

Right: Cartoon from the invitation to the President's Dinner, Dr. Ozmon

Frosh Week,1990s

Then come a few glorious weeks when the campus is warm and sunny and nobody has a care in the world.

But the weather doesn't last, nor does the calm. Time speeds up, mid-terms flash by and exams are looming.

Above: Hitting the books

Left: Then exam schedules go up.

Below: First examination in The Tower, December 1988

Left: Working in the Patrick Power Library

Convocation

Convocation is the end of a journey, a time to celebrate with friends and family, to pray perhaps, and to receive that hard-earned parchment. Since the move to McNally, May Convocation has moved from the Theatre Auditorium to the Lord Nelson Hotel, then the Alumni Arena and finally the Metro Centre. In October 1990, the tradition of a second fall Convocation was revived after an hiatus of 20 years, first in the Theatre Auditorium, then in The Tower.

Right: Communion in the Chapel prior to 1971

Far right: Lighting the candles at the Baccalaureate Service, 1990

Below: The walk to Canadian Martyrs' Church for the Baccalaureate Service

Some of the 20,000 people who have graduated from Saint Mary's since the move to Robie Street in 1951

Background: Amatus Forsac (BSc '96, MBA '98) from Cameroon and his proud family

Left to right:

Heather Nelson graduated in 1991.

In 1976, basketball star and coach Mickey Fox received his degree from Bishop Colin Campbell.

Two Muslim graduates

MLA David Hendsbee was Valedictorian in 1982, when Anne Murray received an honorary degree.

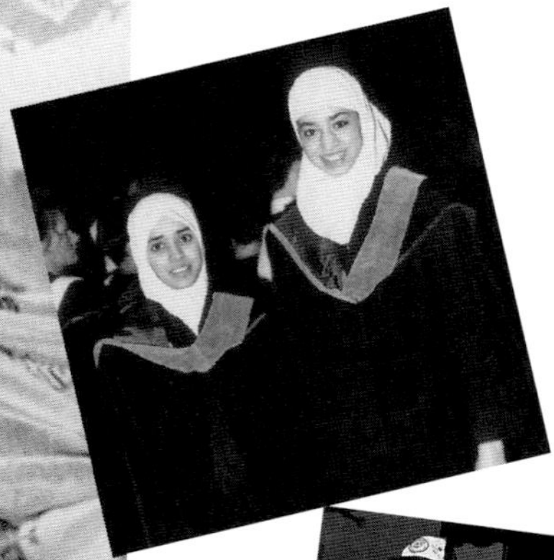

A typical graduating class in the Metro Centre

Honorary degree recipients

Eclectic is the best word to describe the wide range of distinguished people who have been awarded honorary degrees by Saint Mary's over the years. They range from authors, actors and musicians to politicians, scientists, academics and business leaders. In all, 222 people have graduated from Saint Mary's *honoris causa*.

Left, clockwise from top:

Astronaut Roberta Bondar, 1992

Rick Hansen, 1993

Chief Ovide Mercredi, 1992

Left: Prime Minister John Diefenbaker, 1958

Below: Governor General Georges P. Vanier, 1966

Left: Anne Murray, 1982

Below: *Halifax Herald* cartoonist Bruce MacKinnon, 1996

Below: Hank Snow, *in absentia,* 1994

Left: Rita MacNeil, 1989

Below: Irish President Mary McAleese, 1998

Below : Maureen Forrester with President Owen Carrigan, 1972

Behind the scenes

Wherever it is held, Convocation is a huge project, but under the able generalship of Registrar Dr. Elizabeth A. Chard and her army of volunteers it runs like clockwork. Many staff and faculty members play their roles for years and become part of the tradition themselves.

Left: The Dance Decoration Committee played an important role in 1976.

Below, left to right:

Registrar Elizabeth Chard signing parchments

Father William Stewart, SJ leading the procession in 1998. He carried the mace from its inception in 1980 until 1997.

Associate Registrar Murray Wilson ironing flags

Chancellor Archbishop Austin-Emile Burke confers a degree at the 1998 Spring convocation.

Teaching and Learning

In the classroom something magic happens: not immediately or easily, but eventually as this 1961 *Journal* cartoon by Murray Napier describes. The following photo essays about students and their professors try to capture this *Pilgrim's Progress*.

Above: Three deans, end of the 20th cenury: L to R: Dean of Commerce Dr. Paul Dixon, Dean of Arts Dr. Mike Larsen and Dean of Science Dr. David Richardson

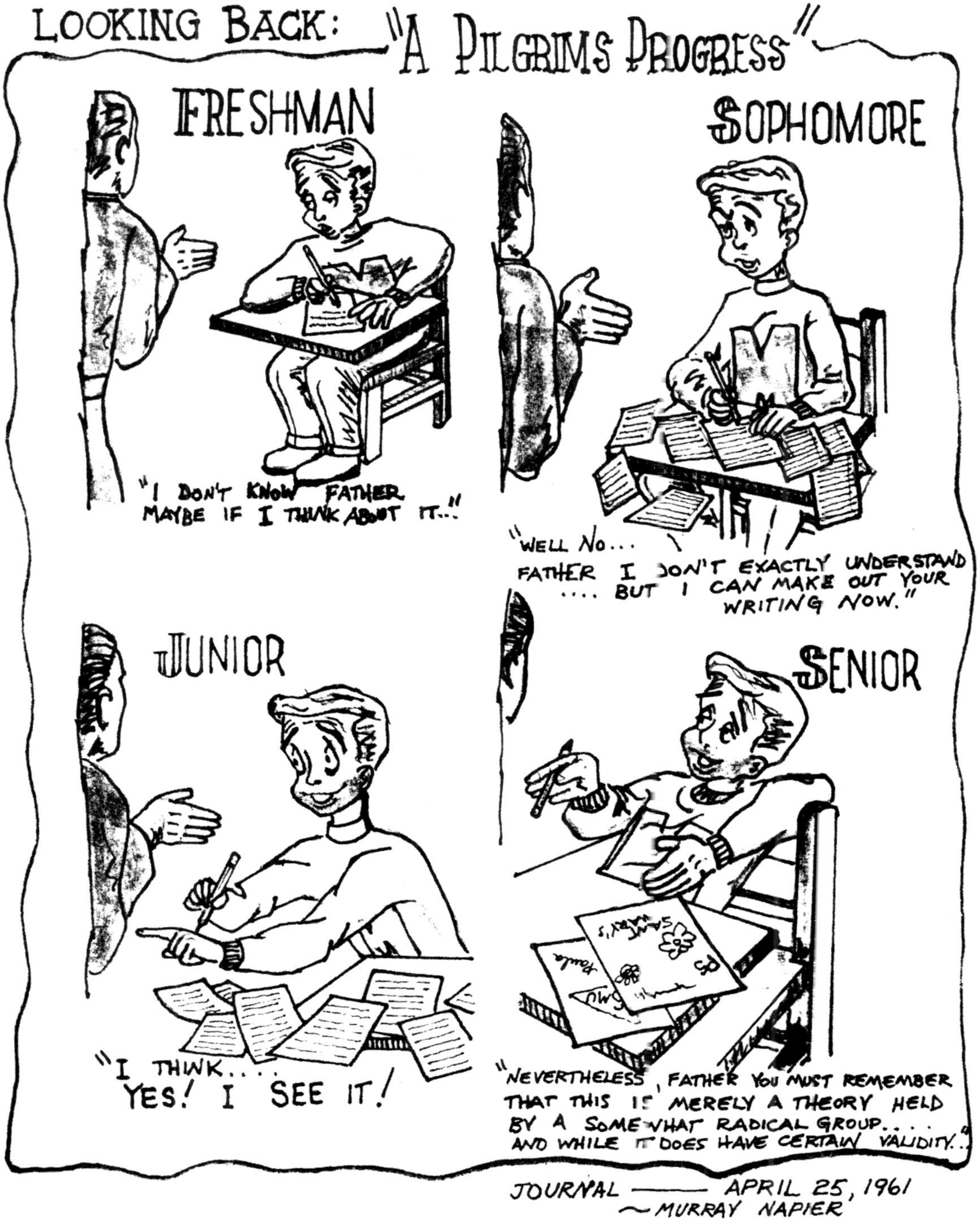

The arts

Father William Stewart, SJ, who taught philosophy on campus from 1950 until retirement, believed the heart of university education is "the development of understanding" through a liberal arts education. Today, the arts and social sciences are taught by a dedicated team which continues the rigorous traditions established by the Irish Christian Brothers and the Jesuit Fathers.

Geography professor Dr. Peter Ricketts and student Sherry Wittman on a field trip, 1981

Professor George Burpee Hallett teaching English

Below: In 1987, Philosophy professor Dr. Peter March introduced "Busking with a Philosopher," which took philosophy out of the classroom and into many new venues including the Dartmouth waterfront and local newspapers.

Right: A 1984 anthropology class explored Halifax of the 18th Century. Standing: Katie Cottreau (Project Mgr), Barb Bishop (assistant). Seated: Mike Simmons, Ann Hiltz, Susan Crowe, Mary Anne Hogan, Tom Craig, Kathy Dawson, Bob Roe, Carol King.

Over the years many interdisciplinary programs and special institutes have been added to the core subjects to meet changing times and interests. These include the Institute of Human Values (1978), Criminology (1975), the Gorsebrook Institute for Atlantic Canada Studies (1982), Asian Studies (1982) and the D'Arcy McGee Chair of Irish Studies (1986)

Right: Classics professor Dr. Geraldine Thomas teaches a small group in her book-lined office.

Below: Anthropology professor Dr. Paul Erickson introduces students to the human skeleton.

Right: Political Science professors Dr. Louise Arseneault (Speaker) and Dr. Don Naulls conducted a mock parliament in Province House, Nova Scotia's historic House of Assembly, in 1994.

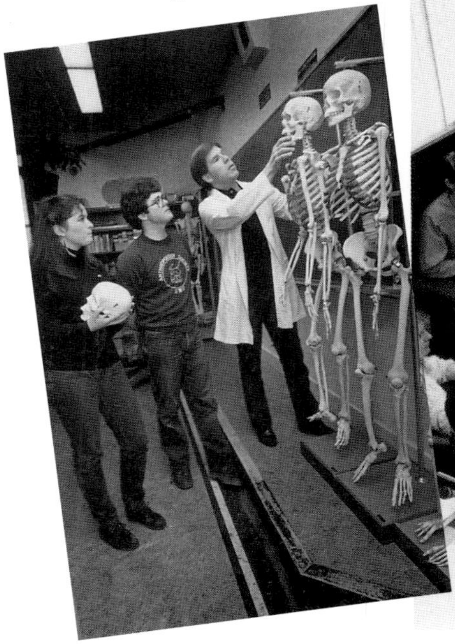

Commerce

Saint Mary's first recognized the importance of commerce to our region in 1840, when it promoted the teaching of European languages to would-be merchants. In 1934, a Bachelor of Commerce degree was first offered. In 1959, Saint Mary's electronic digital computer, the first in the region, was made available to local industry.

Above: The Business Development Centre opened in the Burnside Industrial Park in 1989, its dual purpose to teach students by providing an advisory service for business.

Below: Dr. Tony Charles, Finance and Management Science and Environmental Science

Left: Computers became an essential part of the classroom experience in the 1990s. Dr. Janet Gregory, Finance and Management Science

Right: Professor Nicky Young teaches an MBA class.

Left: Finance and Management Science professor and well-known jazz musician Dr. Harvey Millar

The MBA Program was launched in 1974 and the Executive MBA in 1990. The BComm became a four-year program in 1977 and acquired a Co-op option in 1989. The department became the Frank H. Sobey Faculty of Commerce in 1993 and moved into its state-of-the art building in 1998. In 2000, the first candidates were enrolled in a doctoral program in Business Administration.

Right: First Executive MBA class, 1990

Joyful Bachelor of Commerce alumni of Saint Mary's celebrate becoming chartered accounting professionals. Dr. Frank Dougherty, Accounting, on left.

Below: The SMU Commerce Society has long been a strong force on campus and hosts a Businessmen's Dinner each year. This is the 1976 team.

Science

The Irish Christian Brothers introduced an Engineering Diploma in 1916 and the Faculty of Engineering was created in the 1940s. Until 1967, Saint Mary's granted a BSc under its Faculty of Arts and Science. In that year, the Faculty of Science was born. In 1995, the first Bachelor of Environmental Studies in a Halifax university was established.

Dr. Gary Welch, Astronomy and Physics, teaching inside the observatory

Right: Astronomy with computers. Dr. David Clarke, Astonomy and Physics, 1990s

Left: Dr. Kate Mailer, Chemistry

Below: Dr. John Young, Chemistry

Undergraduate student researchers

Undergraduate science students at Saint Mary's are encouraged to take part in the wide range of research projects undertaken by faculty members, an experience which has equipped many of them to go on to the best graduate schools in the world.

Below left: Dr. David Hope Simpson (R), Geologist. first recipient of the Father William Stewart, SJ Medal for Teaching

Right: Dr. Bill Bridgeo, Chemistry

Below: Physics students working with the mysterious equipment atop Loyola

Above: Engineering students in action

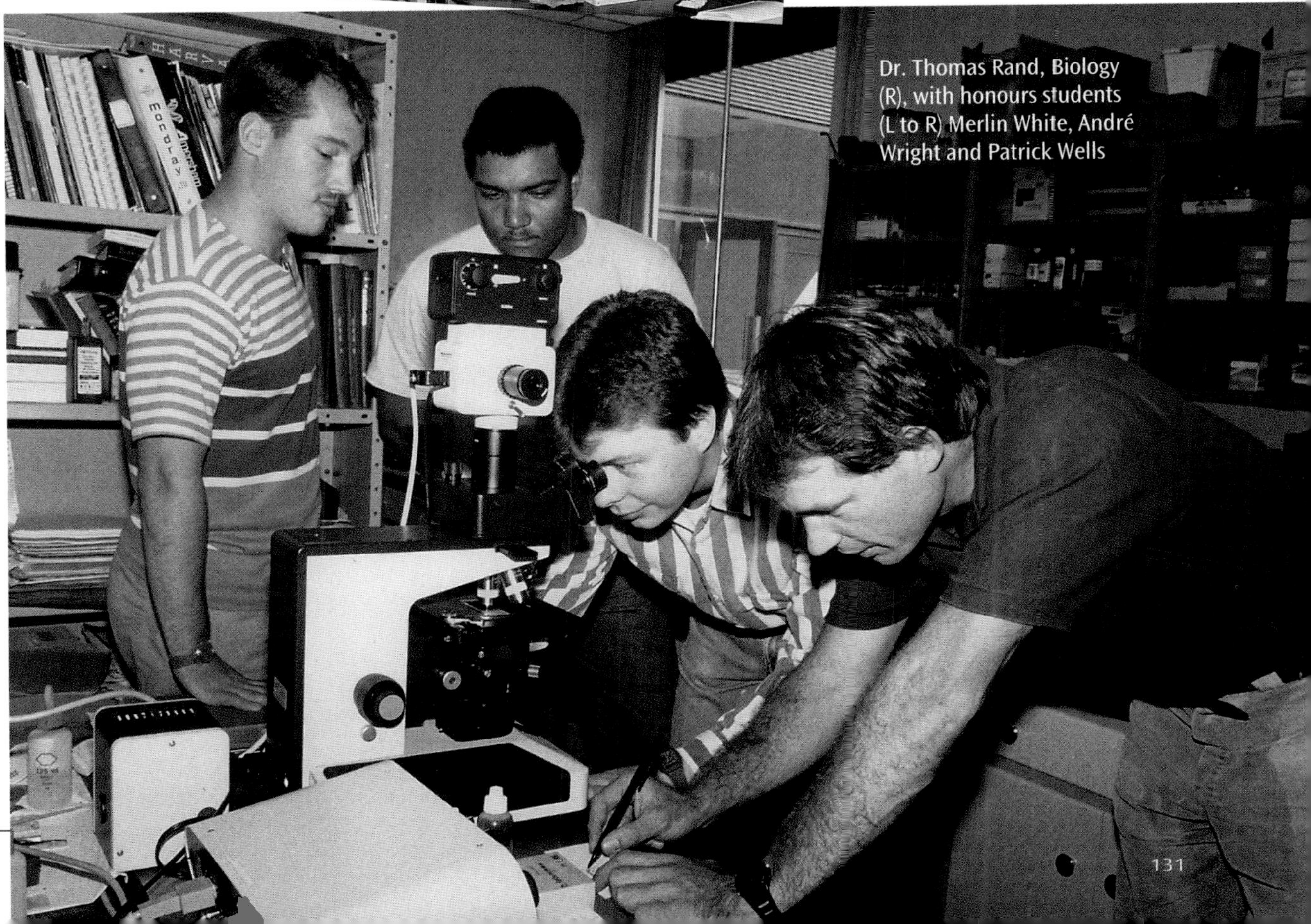

Dr. Thomas Rand, Biology (R), with honours students (L to R) Merlin White, André Wright and Patrick Wells

Teaching teachers

The School of Education was established in 1957, later becoming the Faculty of Education. Its one-year Bachelor of Education program admitted students who had a prior degree and focused chiefly on junior- and senior-high teaching. The MEd was much in demand by practising teachers, for whose convenience many classes were taught in locations outside Halifax, including Truro, Bridgewater and Charlottetown. In the interests of government-mandated "rationalization," the faculty ceased to admit new students in 1994.

Student teacher Allen Wentworth with An Nghiam and Steven Thai.

Left: Education graduate Lisa Harrington teaching from *Science Plus*, a new science course published in 1991. Dr. John Haysom was one of its authors.

Right: Practice teachers' reception in 1973. Dr. Donald Weeren is second from left.

Below: Education class, 1987/88.

Campus Life

The area bounded by Robie and Inglis streets, Tower Road and Gorsebrook Avenue is a micro-world: a vibrant, exciting place peopled by students from many nations and many backgrounds. Some are older, and for some disabilities mean that the educational journey has an extra challenge. It is impossible to reflect on every aspect of campus life, but the following pages will bring back some memories.

So you lived in residence?

For many this is the first time away from home; there is a lot to learn, and many new friends to learn it with.

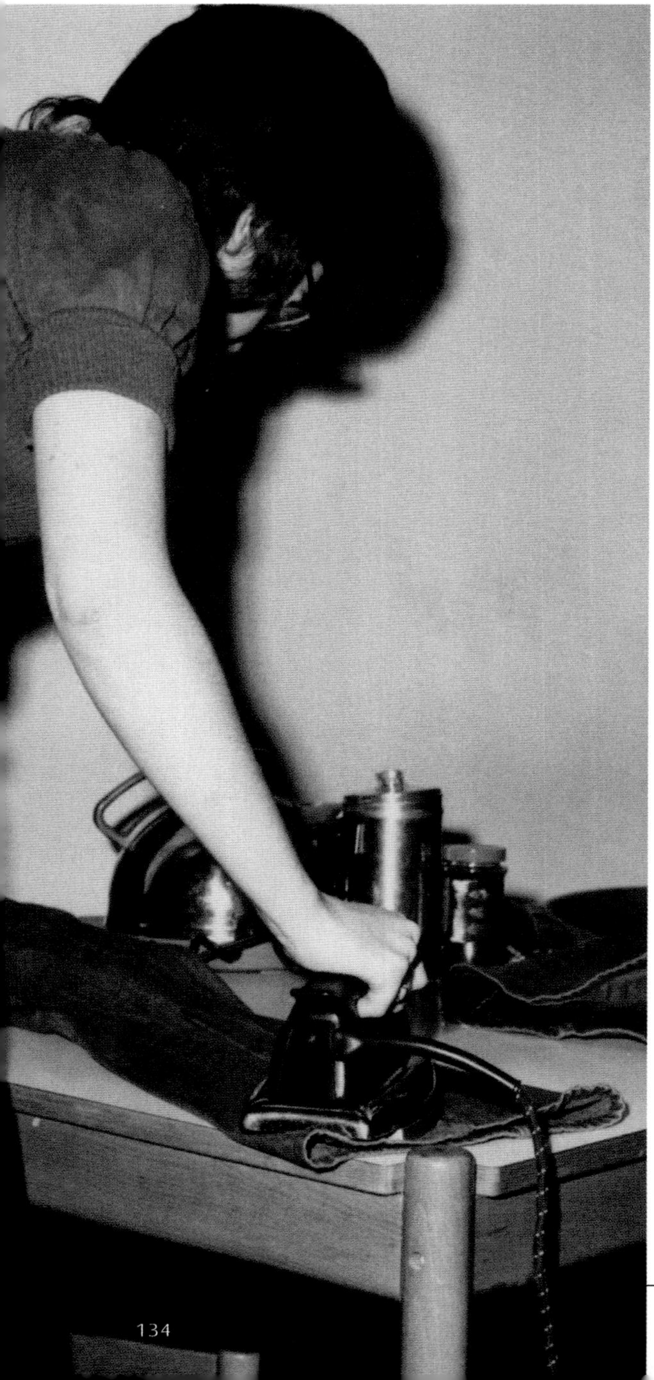

This page:
Left: Ironing those flared jeans, 1960s or 2001?

Right: Student art in the tunnel between Loyola and Rice

Centre: Womens' residence room

Below: Residence dons with (centre L to R) Asst. Residence Director Clay Fowler, Father J.J. Hennessy, SJ (who lived in residence) and Residence Director Keith Hotchkiss, 1978

Opposite page:
Top right: Men's residence room

Centre: Laundry—where's Mom?

Bottom right: Beauty parlour

Far right: Phoning home

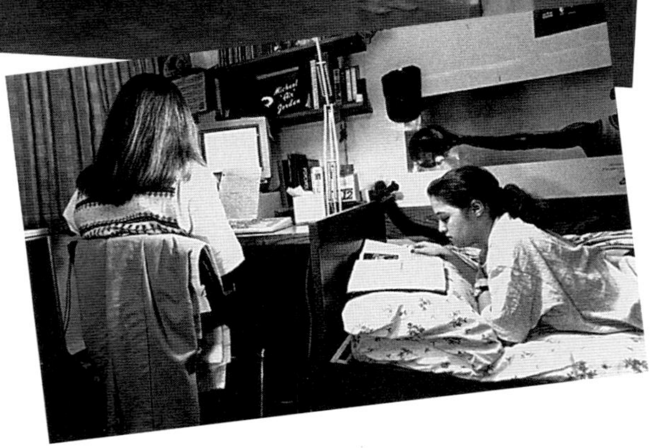

SAINT MARYS

and you had a good time!

Life on campus wasn't all housekeeping and study.

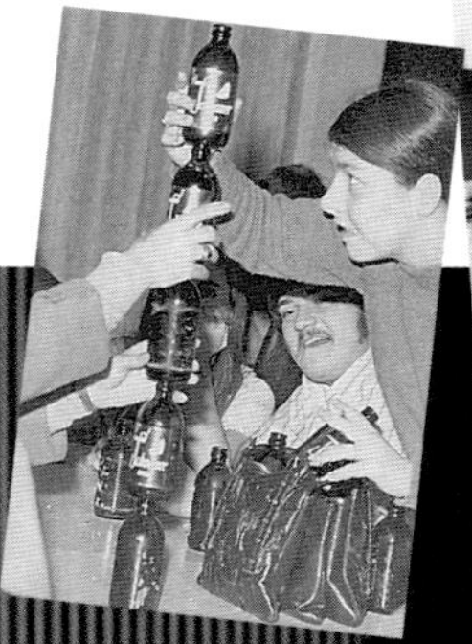

The Gorsebrook Lounge. In its early days Anne Murray, Salome Bey, Jessie Winchester, Mat Minglewood and Dutchie Mason sang there. It is, of course, located in what was sometimes known as the Strident Union Building.

Opposite page, inset L to R:
Many of the most popular non-Olympic sports involved beer!

The "Caps" championship, definitely in the non-Olympic category

Pinball machines in the Student Centre.

This page:
Below: Pool was a popular pastime for some.

Bottom: Winter carnival 1986 involved pie throwing.

Below centre: Preparing Saint Mary's float for the October 1975 Joseph Howe Festival, sadly long defunct

Bottom centre: These politically incorrect guys were contestants in the Male Beauty Contest at Winter Carnival 1986. Meet Lulu and her sisters Lulu, Lulu, Lulu and Lulu.

Right: Things got more formal as graduation rolled around. Cathy MacNeil and Brian Duffy danced the night away at the 1973 Convocation Ball.

Mature students add a different perspective

For many, University is an experience that has had to wait and may have to be fitted in part-time round a demanding career or job. These students are renowned for being keener beaners and tend to obtain high marks. Career upgrading, a long held ambition or just a few non-credit courses, all are equally important.

Right from top to bottom:
Getting the hang of computers

Mature student

Even registration is a bit more tricky with kids in tow.

Mature and part-time students have had their own association at Saint Mary's since 1982. In the early 1990s, its name changed to OPTAMUS (Organization of Part-time and Mature University Students).

The Division of Continuing Education moved into its own home at 883 Robie Street in 1994.

Above: Graduation is such a triumph!

Right: Is this Saint Mary's oldest graduate? Samuel Murdock, seen here with the Dean of Arts' ever-caring secretary Joan Whitney, graduated with a BA in Political Science in October 1992 at age 86.

Below: RCMP officer on campus for class

Reaching out to students with disabilities

Since the 1960s, Saint Mary's has responded to the needs of students with disabilities, and in 1985, the Atlantic Centre of Research, Access and Support for Students with Disabilities opened. Its initiatives have included the Ferguson Tape Library, the Kurzweil reading machines, note takers and support for students with learning disabilities. Other programs have included interpreting for the deaf in the classroom, the training of sign language interpreters and helping students with disabilities find jobs (Making the Employment Connection).

The campus is fully accessible, including Braille signage in elevators.

Left: Paul Gouett, who made his home on campus for a number of years

Below left: Neville Smith graduated with a BSc in Psychology in 1989. He found work through the Employment Connection.

Bottom: The Ferguson Tape Library

Below right: Joanne Hutchinson graduated in 1992.

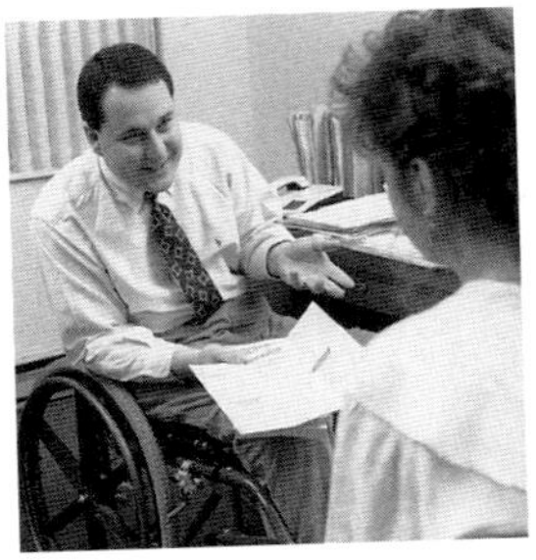

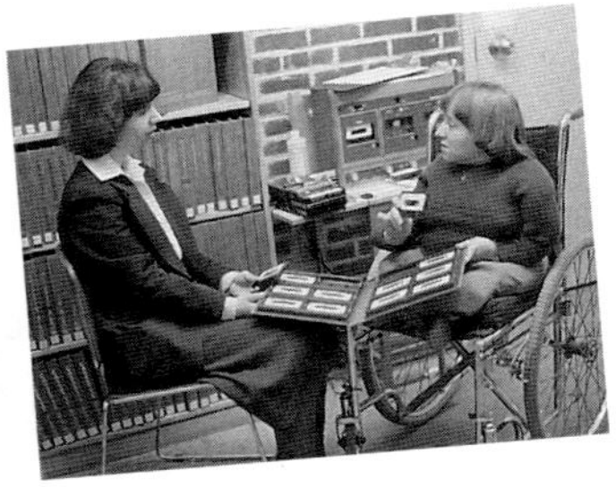

Deaf student Deborah Robar was Valedictorian in 1989. All Convocations are signed for the deaf.

Penny Kitchen studied at Saint Mary's in 1987–88 with the support of the Atlantic Centre.

Diane Fletcher, who is deaf, taught American Sign Language to would-be interpreters.

Bryan Levangie (Co-op Commerce) appreciated the help of a large print computer, text magnifying machine and other support services.

The launch of the Employment Connection in 1989 with Atlantic Centre Director David Leitch at the podium

A small world

In 2002, over 12 per cent of students on campus are from outside Canada. This trend has been growing for many years as Saint Mary's has built strong links with countries around the world. It is also a Saint Mary's tradition to welcome refugee students through the World University Services Canada (WUSC) program. International students often participated in programs of the International Education Centre (1972–1995) and their presence gave rise to the Teaching English as a Second Language program.

Below bottom: East Indian student Sarada Vankamamidi performed in the Art Gallery in 1989 • Below top: Japanese New Year celebrations, 1995

Below: In 1986, the Saint Mary's Chinese Students' Association celebrated Chinese New Year with its 15th annual banquet. The Dragon Dance was one of many highlights.

Centre, clockwise:

Chinese students (L to R) Janet Chan, Amy Chan and Selina Ng in costume, for the Lantern Dance, 1987

Students from the Hokkaido Musashi Women's Junior College in Sapporo, Japan, performed the Yosakoi-Soran Dance during their stay on campus.

African Night: Kike Belo and Irene Kyompaire in a dance called Pata Pata

Right, top to bottom:

L to R: Eritrean students Ephram Abraha and Amanuel Negassi Abrha and Ugandan Sam Kezekiya came to Saint Mary's through the WUSC Refugee Student program.

Professor Barbara Davison teaching English as a Second Language, 1991

Ethiopian students from Mount Saint Vincent University at African Night in 1993

Bottom, left to right:

African Night brings out colourful and elegant costumes—
L to R: Catherine Adesanya, Phil Okeke and Rose Tchwenko, 1993.

Activities in the International Education Centre

They trod the boards at Saint Mary's

Drama was a tradition at Saint Mary's College under the Irish Christian Brothers. In 1959, the Jesuits established the Saint Mary's University Drama Society, affectionately known as SMUDS. Before Neptune Theatre opened, there was little live theatre in Halifax, and students performed to packed houses. For many years, the volunteer team which supported this venture consisted of Father William Stewart, SJ, moderator; Faith Ward, director; Anthony Law and Jane Shaw, scenery artists; and Doris Butters, wardrobe mistress.

Left: *The Importance of Being Earnest*, 1979. Dominic Larkin (Algernon) and Anita Price (Cecily).

Inset left: Jari-Matti Helpi, Carol ?, Ken Storey, Joanne Hagen, Dominic Larkin.

Below left: *Dangerous Liaisons,* 1990.

Below right: *Arsenic and Old Lace*, 1974 L to R: Derek Ashton, Deborah Allen, Darcel Mailaix. Deborah Allen is a professional actor and in 2001, "starred" as Dame Judi Dench's stand-in in *The Shipping News.*

Above: *Rozencrantz and Guildenstern are Dead*, 1971. Brian Tardiff (L) and Tony Johnstone

They also serve who only work backstage

Top right: Paul Gilles gets help with *Macbeth* from Super Bill, SMUDS Moderator (for that read mentor, stagehand, painter, carpenter and more) Father William Stewart, SJ. Super Bill's first apron went missing, so the cast got him number two.

Centre right: Makeup, 1976

Right: Behind the scenes: the stage in the Old Gym, which was under the Theatre Auditorium

Below: Setting up the lights for a production of *Death Trap* in 1985

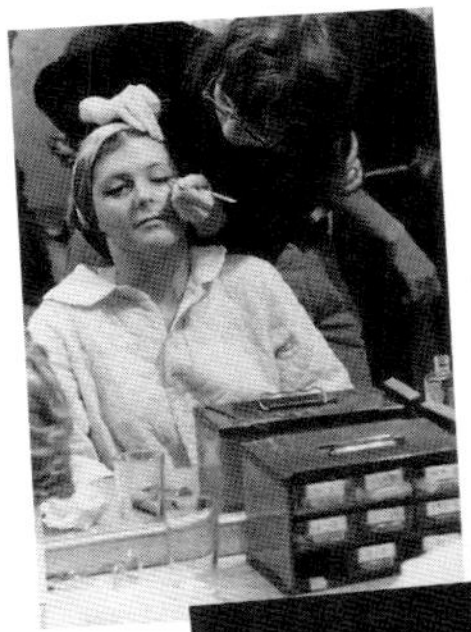

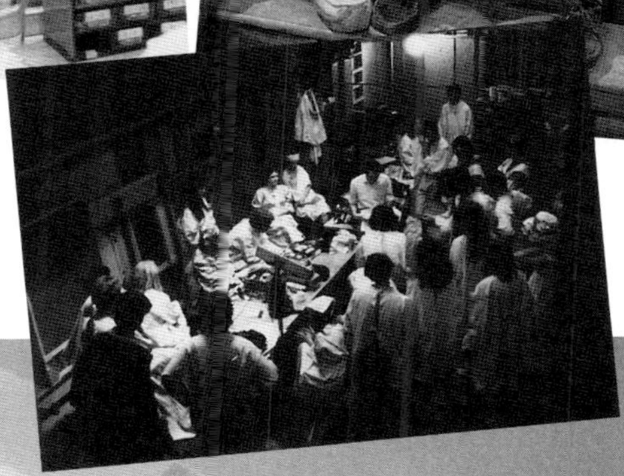

Right: *Pride and Prejudice*, 1983. L to R: n/k, Rob Casey (Mr. Darcy), Claire Milton (Elizabeth Bennett)

Right: 1978 A curious scene from *Inside Outside Alice*, a commentary on *Alice in Wonderland*

Below: *The Taming of the Shrew*, 1973. Magnificent set by artist and Art Gallery Director Anthony Law

Staff

Without the essential staff who make the wheels go round, there would be no smooth-running institution. These unsung heroes tend to stay at Saint Mary's for a long time and will be remembered by many of you.

1988: a rare break in the sun for hard working Physical Plant staff. L to R: Clem Rodrigues, Phil MacDonald, Frank Gerbaz, Murray Martin, Sheldon Glick and Ben Slauenwhite

Right: Earl Surette and Marion Lecky at the 1978 grand opening of the Mini Mart, which has now disappeared. Earl joined Saint Mary's in the early 1970s when the store was next to the Beauty Parlour and is still serving students.

Below left: Bookstore Manager Don Harper in 1989

Bottom left: Telephone operator Pauline Fougere, seen here in 1987, could do 10 things at once. A bouquet of red roses marked her 30 years of service in 1991.

Below centre: Chef Ray Wincey preparing 20 gallons of gravy for Christmas Dinner in 1985

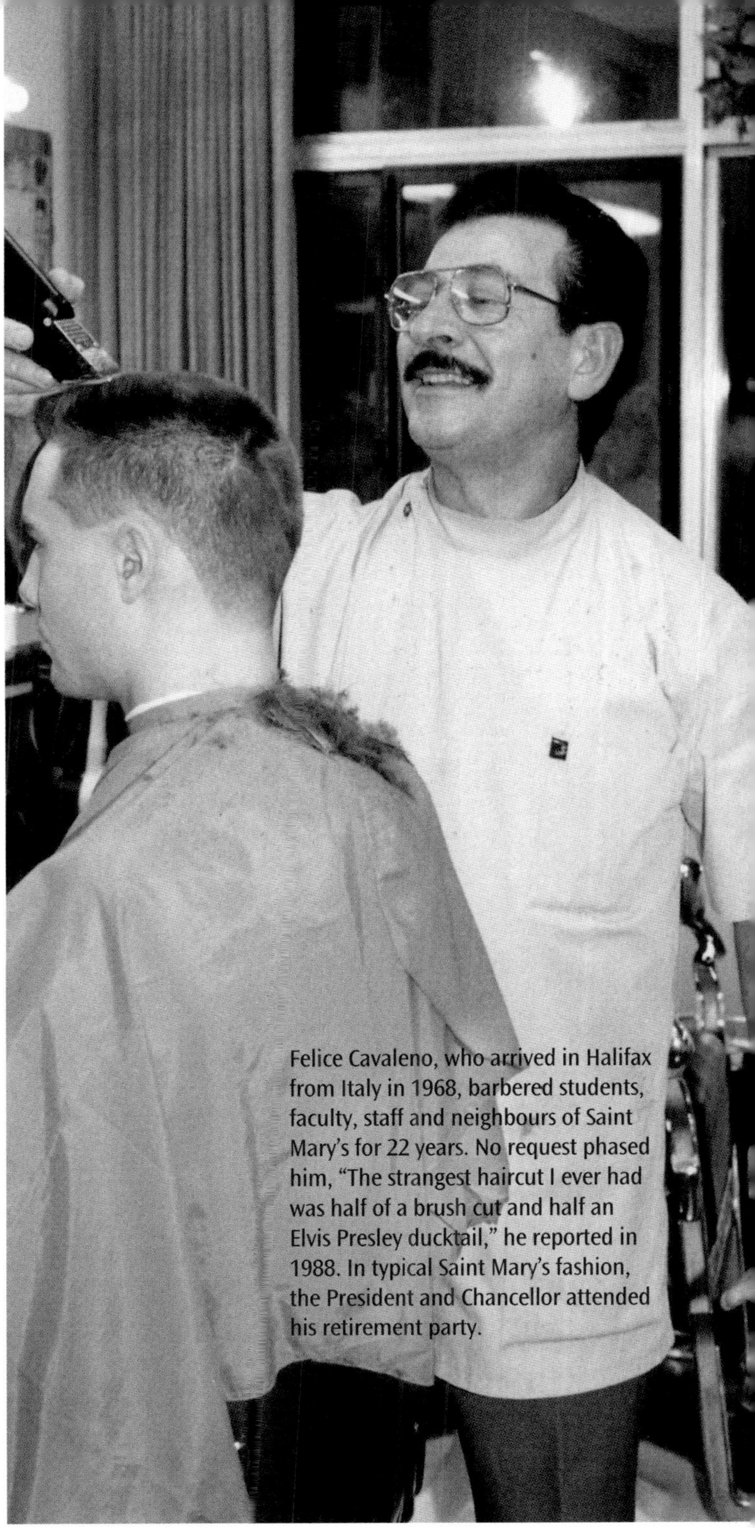

Felice Cavaleno, who arrived in Halifax from Italy in 1968, barbered students, faculty, staff and neighbours of Saint Mary's for 22 years. No request phased him, "The strangest haircut I ever had was half of a brush cut and half an Elvis Presley ducktail," he reported in 1988. In typical Saint Mary's fashion, the President and Chancellor attended his retirement party.

The art gallery

There is always something exciting going on at the gallery and the annual Faculty, Staff and Student Art Exhibition is a popular annual highlight.

Students study an exhibition of pre-Colombian pottery.

1988: Student Fiona Lotz and her son Peter examine David Bobier's sculpture of a skeleton bathtub in an exhibition entitled *Domestic Effects*.

Long-time Artist in Residence Leighton Davis mounts an exhibition.

Saint Mary's first and second Artists in Residence, Robert Dietz (L) and Anthony Law. These two fine artists shared a strange bond. During the Second World War, Robert Dietz served in the German army, while Anthony Law commanded a Motor Torpedo Boat in the Canadian navy.

A Family Affair

Despite its current enrolment of around 7,500 students (full- and part-time), Saint Mary's tries to retain the family atmosphere which goes back to its days as a small college for Roman Catholic young men. Many students have watched their children and grandchildren graduate, while others have found their niche in the University and served until retirement.

Stephanie Cleary attended her first convocation in 1966 with her father Kevin Cleary, who served the University in many capacities and retired as Secretary to Senate in 1999. All five Cleary children attended Saint Mary's, and Stephanie, now a Crown Attorney in Medicine Hat, graduated in 1986.

Previous page: The Dodds family. Dr. Colin Dodds became Saint Mary's 35th President in 2000. L to R: Lizzie, Colin, Carol and James. Above: Lizzie Dodds enjoyed meeting Santa Claus (Father William Stewart, SJ) at the children's Christmas party in 1986.

Above: Long time Chemistry Professor Dr. Keith Vaughan proudly poses with his son Andrew, also a chemist, at his graduation in 1995.

Left: Alumnus and long-serving Chairman of the Board Ron Downie presents the University Medal to his daughter Liane at Convocation in 1989.

Above: In 1971, Leonara Marrigan and her son Michael graduated together. Leonara's MA thesis was an excellent study of Bishop Edmund Burke.

"Pleasant Miss Janet Pottie maintains pleasant public relations" was the caption under this photo (left) in the 1957 *Santamarian*. Janet Pottie was Saint Mary's first public relations director. Her daughter Suellen Murray (above), now a lawyer, studied PR at The Mount and worked in the Public Relations Department in 1986.

Even visitors come in families. Paul Martin Senior (right) visited the campus in 1966 and Finance Minister Paul Martin Junior (below), seen here with Political Science professor Dr. Leonard Preyra, was here in 2001.

Here ends our look back over the 200-year story of Saint Mary's University. We have reached the present—where tradition meets the future.

Left: Lisa Legatto, current editor of the University newspaper *The Times*, treasures a photograph of her grandfather John Patrick Floyd: He attended the High School and this photo was probably taken in 1934, his first year at the College.

Alumnus Lou Cuccia presented the Dow Chemical scholarship to his daughter Mary Cuccia in 1983.